Winds of Change

ELIZABETH MARTINA BISHOP

Requests for permission to reproduce selections of this book should be mailed to:

Elizabeth Martina Bishop, Ph.D.
2675 West State Route 89A, #1100
Sedona, AZ 86336, USA

ISBN-13: 978-1499666793
ISBN-10: 1499666799

BISAC: Poetry/General

Design by Artline Graphics, Sedona AZ, USA
www.artline-graphics.com

Original cover artwork by Premdevi Assael,
www.premdeviart.com.

Original interior artwork by Anugito, Artline Graphics.

Winds of Change

ELIZABETH MARTINA BISHOP

BOOK 1 • ENTROPY

BOOK 2 • A MEMOIR PORTFOLIO

BOOK 3 • GRANDMOTHER BIRD

BOOK 4

DINNER WITH THE GREEN TARA
A One Act Verse Play

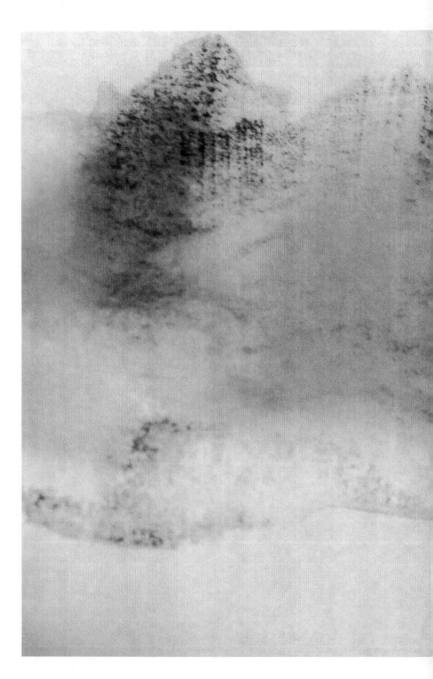

BOOK 1

ENTROPY

Canine

Now they want to study my brow, measure my head.
Tot up the number of sifted bones it takes to construct
A man of very few words and, of late, far fewer words.
And that is what he said. Has he, the anthropologist,
Lost the book of his soul to the small print, to unkind
Words and to the blind caring that is mine, no one else's?
Unprecedented, the number of hunters out to sniff the air,
To tame my blood. When I saw her fall among them,
I lost my mind.
What they really meant, not even intoned in the curling tongue
Of leaf language nor in the blood curdling - cry of foxes
Nor with a forked stick could I even
Divine the sense of my name: Ishi.

I am an absurd cause for truth.
Undeterred, beneath the inky, black wing,
I bite the raven knuckles of my hand.
The rug pulled out from under me.
You understand, don't you, my wife is dead?
Undeterred, I dream dreams of her.

Smoke

Beneath the soles of my barefoot dreams, I burn.
I burn. A while later, I return
With the mockery of a thousand white men.
You must figure out how many meals
I will consume before I die.
You measure days and then you die of pride
That congeals like words on a pewter plate.
Coyotes howl. Lightning decides
The zig zag of cloudless nights.
What does the spirit of the living leaves infer?
They spoke well of you, Ishi, before you died.
You'd never harmed anyone,
Not even a momentary bird that flew past your shoulder
Was able to decide
Why did she die when she was the last one that slept by your side?
Why was the veil of sleep pulled from your eyes?
You never even knew
The man that felled her while she dreamt
Of the ribboned arrows of tenderness
And left you dying and alone,
Unable to pronounce your name.
The workmen in the slaughterhouse did not understand:
How could you pronounce the shaped
Contours of death, pull out the cactus quills, and end your life?
Now you are a specimen of pemmican of their world.

Blemish

Where are you going? You said we would head sunwards
Towards that hill. I do not think we will. At least, not today.
Behind a shallow map of burlap and a sliver of glass,
How can I bear peeling my nails without a Swiss army knife?
Eyeless, the unseen leans towards clairvoyant rivers.
Cloudless, the night sky that stings my dark skin.
With the laughter of the past, a future bride out of reach.
Go ahead, float gold and a sense of garish and gauche deliverance.
Nothing is too old: panning for gold in a River of Change.
If pennies fall into a tin cup, you slump against the wall.
No Moses here.
Now ask: what is the use of using each other while on earth?
The beggared hand extended is like a man's brush with death.
I am like a homeless man on holiday,
A pavee without her children,
A skinny heron standing on one leg.
They say you can imitate
The sound of any bird, even foreign ones,
You've never heard of.

What they said about me:
The sound of any bird,
The sound of a child crying,
Enough said.

Betrayal

There were problems all right. You took me
In a corner and asked me didn't I know
I was a complete failure?
Look at me. Look at me now.
There is no way to keep us alive without lying
About the meaning of scissors, paper plates
Blue lagoons, and knives and forks. The moon is full.
Look more deeply than you have ever looked.
You will have been looking at me for all these years.
You will admit that, haven't you been doing that?
Without really turning inward as a marigold,
Does a field filled with miscreant daisies do the same?
All but asleep at night,
I wander around in my nightgown
Without sensing the remote possibility
Of anything of significance
Ever happening to either one of us.
Perhaps, the animal instinct for survival
Makes you sniff at clouds
As if each cloud contained a message
For gods and goddesses deafened
By the noise of existence
Could you ever bring yourself
To the brink of imagination's precipice?
Though both you and I might be dead
This time next year.
I can say: I can't go on living like this.
I feel the fingers of my grand aunts
Are constantly fingering the brooch

Worn around my neck.
I am not yet convinced of anything
Resembling a betrayal, not yet.
Without truly seeing beyond the wider lens
Of possibility, I am nothing.
If I am a bluebird in a tree of sorrow
Sobbing because you won't return,
In time, know this: I have painted so many pictures
Of you but you still won't speak to me
And you won't come home, not for anything.
I play chopsticks on the piano
While on the other side of the pavilion screen
You look away. You yawn.

Visionary Waitress

Think of it. The waitress on duty
For ten hours on a swing shift.
Didn't she have a caesarean when she was young?
The knife sits in the flesh among make believe scars.
The spirit of the dead child upon her.
You never get over a thing like that.
A nightgown soaked in blood.
Love grown stale as the last crust
Of bread offered to a dying man,
The one she took care of for a time,
The man dressed in a blood spattered bib.
Cherokee tears shed before what indifferent altar?
Her history is not his history.
Is it the year of the bear or the year of the gnat?
You could make a memory map
Of the entire world with little stick pins in a table mat.
Her feet hurt. Her moccasins worn thin
Beyond the call of duty. It's a no win situation
For the Cherokee Braves. You must be kidding
Not again! Not another loss!
The good red road, almost a forgotten orphan.
Worse than those chancers performing the stomp dance
All the way across Oklahoma in the Trail of Tears,
Her sneakers sweat as if she has never worked for less.
No gold stars pinned on blouses
For princesses of sweat lodges and alms-houses.
Princesses. When she gets home,
She dips her hands in rainwater,
She drinks coffee from a paper cup.

Longing

Now I know why I miss you.
If I say I have been thinking
Of you all night I would be lying.
I know once in a while I would not.
When gnats flit above skyscrapers
Like souls on errands
In a new country of swans
They come and go
Now I am no longer angry.
How could I be?
I could have skipped this part of my life so easily.
I'm an ocean away in a place that has
And in a new hat that has multiple
I wonder what the art exhibits
Will look like? I want to be who I am.
And yes, I know I left two children behind.
But, so what!
The porcelain bowls
In the sideboard cupboard
Shine in a resplendent dalliance of absence.
Heart valves pump with a difference
On these cobblestone walks.
Once I was single-minded,
Now I'll take any path.
I'll dodge the dropping light at dusk.
What keeps me old is the same thing
That kept me wedded to Benares, my old hangout.

Poem for Pema Chodron

Everyone wants to help.
Please take my hat. Please take
Everything I own. The rose in the decanter
Is not enough. Please take my prayer mat.
After that, my coat. If I am privileged enough
To choose to be dispossessed, take my spirit too.
At best, all is not lost. Failing this,
Please take my best dress shirt.
Dissolve the little stripes in it, one by one,
Into a wide expanse of lapis lazuli from Dehra Dun.
Why as an outcaste spirit,
Must I fear love's inane reproach?
In order to breathe in
Compassion's milk,
I look up at the stars
The planetary alignments
Of Mars Saturn and beyond
Are truly marvelous at this time.
I am vexed that I do not know
What you will ask me to do next.
Must I now learn to drop coppers
In a wicked paper cup and lie?

Doors

Are taken for granted by those who know how to walk
Without inhaling the pale blue color of whirling blue stars
And blue horses that crowd the lens of those pilgrims
Seeking metaphors about the need for woodpeckers
That break their beaks on doors of consciousness.

Marigolds Turning Inwards

While asleep, I heard that marigolds
In the wake of morning had somehow agreed
To trade in the color of joy as proof positive
Of something illogical, indecipherable, and irrational.
Something out of reach in the way of an altar.
Fuchsia pales before and then afterwards decides
To take another pathway without telling anyone
About the cosmic epicenter and what it means.
Why fret over earth's cosmic make over?
Now the cowslip obediently obliges to change
The color of dusk grew on the pathway to the forest.
By growing under the lip of a leaf and then letting go
In a burst of spring color, I have heard the nettles
Wading deep in the field. Upon hearing the corncrake
Entering in a portal, the noiseless sound of daisies
That correlated every petal with other types of bird song.

Careless Moon

Why should I lean into the moon
In careless caress and swoon of light?
Whose oversight, a thankless cry
Of recognition from Brother Raven,
Whose oversight?
The mapping of this Walpurgis Night?
If he the one chosen to throw the dice,
Now shrouded and occluded
By smoke plumes the size of palm trees,
I wonder when the all clear signal
Will be finally shrouded or sounded.
At that time, will quail as well as cousins
Emerge from cloud cover omnipotent and clever
And once again quaff a cup of bitters
Held up in offering by a sacrosanct Mother Earth?
Why collude with wings of uneasy silence?
Though clipped and pruned the foliage on the path,
I find it even more bewildering than my love.
Were it true, I love myself as much as you,
When the moon agrees withdraw
The comb of ocean from a comely tomb,
My heartbeat might serve as a stand in
For someone more fervently passionate,
And rare. If plumes of smoke were lovers,
I'd count so many in my endless circle
I might decide I'd remain friendless all my life.

Trivial Pursuit

SHE SAID:
I must rinse my hair.

HE SAID:
It is so nice to have someone to talk to.

SHE SAID:
Are you aware the tone of your voice would wake the dead?

HE SAID:
Nice talking to you. I remember talking to your father about
the dead man's float. The joy of sex.

SHE SAID:
I must wash the dishes. I know my flotilla of bubbles are grotesque,
but still.

HE SAID:
I cook my own meals. I don't wash other people's dishes. Oh, one
of your hands looks bloody awful.

SHE SAID:
I slit my wrist. Now I must rinse my hair.

HE SAID:
Why not write a sonnet instead? You always wrote fetching sonnets.
One day I might try a few.

SHE SAID:

I live inside of my head. Do you want another slice of buttered toast or bread? Now I am not being far fetched, but people doubt my sanity. I wear the wrong clothes you know. There are soubriquets for these kind of people who don't know what to wear, don't know what to say, and don't know what to do. A woman told me her son was chained to another man and swam across a lake. I didn't disbelieve her, but I have always doubted her ability as regards mediumship and her inner convictions as regards truth. I want to be open to all kinds of conversation. Yet I fear the venal sin of repercussion.

HE SAID:

I am a political animal. I know full well man also is. Keynes said this and a few other economists.

SHE SAID:

And a few others. Do you want a table napkin?

HE SAID:

Why do you always boil things down to domestic niceties and games of trivial pursuit?

Bidding you Farewell

However it is
The wind has to untie from the tree
Its most precious birds
Unclasping ankle bracelets
That held you here
Why hold fast
To the soul's earthen prison?
Love's timeless tokens endlessly mistaken
Her immortal cyphers
Only these shaken leaves
Memory disowns
An unopened letter,
The pen of unknown scribes: unwritten silence.
Who is carrying that grain of wheat?
When someone told me of your spirit
Passing, your soul fled into the wind of waking
The spent flight of a thousand birds burned
All your words
Had you lived,
Your presence,
Would it have changed
The history of the mind?
The history of the world ran out of time.
Before the altar of the snowy owl
Addresses all her relatives
I will tear the sermon from a tree branch.
What have I to say anyway?
Was I the one
Who wanted to tarry

Before the memory
Of a lost embrace?
Was I a potrait of a steadfast Noah on a tidal wave?
What you say to me now
Is translated between two worlds.
Your face has changed the faces of seers and pilgrims.
Dear one, you do not know me now
Tied and untied
Within the ample wind of spirit
Wampum's imprisoned seeds let fly the poison fire
A swatch of antique lace
A patchwork coverlet.
Said to be of no particular value
How will a gemstone
Make any difference?
Why am I suspicious of the soul's origin?
Whatever I say about your passing
I never earned your love
The innocent thumbprints of the moon are buried.
The spent music
Time's tethered fire
I asked god why must I part with your garden
I promised never to reveal
The imperiled presence of the owner
The soul's inner space
Despite my fear of death
Among us she is walking
Quickening her step.
Among us she is coming

How have we come to know of her
Surrounded as we are in ignorance of our faith?
Clothed in buffalo robes
Among us she is coming
Swooning in a white clouds of witness
She is coming
She is coming
We tell ourselves
We believe in her.
White Buffalo Calf Woman.

Waiting for the Thunder Beings

Why do we wait for healing?
Healing can take place today.
Though this day nearly over,
And the dark night endless,
The need for rain is measureless.
What silences each raindrop before it falls?
A tall order to delight in proverbs,
While drought and thirst makes us pale.
Faces seem to sicken and we fall poorly sick.
Waste not, want not!
That's what the old people,
Clothed in polka dotted handkerchiefs,
And regal head dresses have always said.
All day, we continue to play chess
Hoping a fickle wind will die down
With a chaste recklessness.
What reminds us of jaded jackdaws
And wandering minstrels?
Why allow a disowned or mindless frown?
What proves an Indian an Indian?
Everyone else looks away,
While you
Play the drum,
And sacrifice silence.
While arrows drum at your back,
You keep looking for an answer
From the thunder beings.

Bees

Why should be the bee
Agree to become loquacious?.
Scribes have noted that bees are often superstitious
About the disappearance of long horn cattle,
The trumpeting swan, elk and bison
Have been long gone.
Almost paradise,
Who could ask for more?
They are shooting giraffe
And lionesses in zoos
In and out of monsoon season.
We feed on each other's pathetic fallacies
As long as the love nest holds.
Bathos and pathos do as well.
Why eat of forbidden fruit
Shot down by Lilith and then by Eve?
Yet may flowers may not have bloomed
So beautifully in this a season of despair and exile.
The diaspora of the vine,
The disappearing dances
Of the monarch butterfly.
The lack luster appearance
Of the new wine-merchants
Leaving much to be desired.
That should be enough to teach us once and for all.
Classes of prognosticators, prophets, and seers,
Each one should be banned and blamed from elevators.
Too often love has witnessed
Seasons of plenty and penury.

Certain events must be played out
The war of the roses no longer over roses
In the desert everything
Appears drought-ridden
As poison fire assails
The innocent and wise
None can idle in the desert
Without averting their gaze
From the eye of the sun.
Some of us have lived too long
Money slides through your fingers
Like a song,
That's what my mother
Always said.
The school house is nothing
But a charnel house.
So, don't overstay your welcome.

Signs

While eaglets and quail
Stroll around in their prams
In sky-oceans holding fast
Star-gazers infer
Planetary alignments
Shaped by this great emptiness
Or else wind-driven spirits
Hold sway over everything.
If blinded pilgrim eyes
Appearing to blink
But once in the wake
Of fated fire, what then
Of last breath, first breath?
Who can foretell
Or forestall the appearance
Of the great dancer, the Grand Trine
Bearing witness to the idleness of wine-sellers
Fasting on the leavings
Of auctioneer's blocks
Before the deluge of the tsunami hits.
Someone says: prophets of landslides
Should be banned. We do not like
To hear the neighbors talk about such things.
What of the history of the moon?
The moon talks back
Before those shadow-players.
What of the wilderness of fire
Tempered by love witnessing love
Whose storms and famines no longer

Ignite hunger for the divine?
Wherever the wind takes you, -
Heed that journey's song
If the Lorelei and her Minions
Snip the innocent strings of fate
Leaving no sign and no trace
Your spirit ever walked this earth.
A circle of quiet and lonely people,
They too, will be deemed shoplifters.
Did they not deem the birds
Will fly from the golden branches
Everlasting?

Stardom

Desire for stardom
Not a graceful child
After all. Ambushed
And placed in the corner.
No rounded edges
Before the sighing wind.
What sentry box
Do you want to check today?
So, who am I? So, who are you to speak
To topple kingdoms in the sand?
Suddenly you understand nothing
Of words. All words fade away into nothingness.
Craters, stars meteors, pet cats,
Those who have corgis or cats are both liars.
False witnesses may nullify agreements
Or give notice suddenly
For posts that no longer exist
Rescind the imagining of gods and poets
Who bow before pale stars.
What poets usually do at midnight
Is their own business
And the business of pet shop owners.

Nourishment

They give us soup
Made out of chicken and vodka spittle
Will it work wonders for our health?
Ah no, too late my brothers
They've already ordered our death.
Bell-tolled chimes are sounded before kneeling princesses.
To make a near death experience
Seem more arcane, mundane, or pleasing
Please make a little book
With a river running through it.
And stardust for good measure.
This is only a test for mestizo members
Or for those who would enjoy
A cup of matzo ball soup.

Birds Scare More Easily

As a matter of course
He had slept within
Every raftered room
Of the house for years.
One day, while he thought
This the the way
It has always been.
Cuckolded and scolded
By soft tears
Falling round about
Before the sermon of the wind
Had bent the holy aftermath of storms,
He asked:
Why not bathe in moonlight?
Whatever left to drought
In the hereafter
Am I not a servant
Of whirling supernovas
In which I still take delight?
Though I have
No standing ground,
Such as I am,
Why must I travel
Inside myself
Until the balanced halves
Of roofs collide?
Such as I am,
As widower of windows
Must I make amends

For the warm
And needless frame I wear?
Though I am breath
Inside breath
Breath may not disrespect
Or disappear
If my heartbeat quickens.
I know there must be a temple goddess
Somewhere near the river.
Long ago, though I might have rested
In the shadow of the Lord,
I may not have understood
How thirsty
For the taste
Of ripened fruit
That plunged me
Earthward
In the first place.
Were the monkey gods
That courageous
They would know where I would begin
Time's bell-chimed journey
From her laughing womb.
Now and again,
I tell myself
Why fear
The future?
Daylight knows the tumult and the fever
Inhabiting the blood of humans.

Whoever the guests are
I will make good
With their comings and goings.
Whatever force
Fully present,
When the world was made,
Was I ever
Dimly aware
The shape of the wind
The shape of thought
Bent the world
Immediately unattended?
At that point,
I may have been
The one depending
On entering
King Solomon's Mountain.
The truth is:
Water knows the mind of man.
Gleaned
From dark whorls
Of presence.
Crowding the lens
Of third heaven,
Would that render me someone
Willing or unwilling to go it alone?
God, why put me to the test?
At best, one question lingers
Do you want to stay
Inside your cave forever
Or let your spirit fly?
A chickadee
Allows for the delicate stance
Of her twig-like legs

Stayed against the branch
Of exile.
How long does it take to live a life
Of innocent scolding?
Her insolent and innocent dance
Tells me she has suffered long enough.
Full well she knows
Whatever happens,
The eyebrow of an old man
Will neither press or ease her on her way
To other lands
Here a yardstick in the hand
By which to measure
The lives of the great and little ones
Ripening like apricots.
The stems of fallen threads of orchards,
Whatever it was had held us,
Holding us no longer
Upon the iron brim of the world.

Love

Who can silence love?
What does love demand?
Research, my friends?
Endless research,
Boundless research?
No smoke signals from above.

Portrait

The almond tree in the back of the house
Is flooded with passionate blossoms.
True as god, you can almost smell them
Once a guru existed who smelled the contents of letters
Before opening them. But what did that make him?
A savant or a seer or merely a dream-weaver of sorts?
Don't talk back to the dead. Watch what comes
Out of your mouth. O ye sullen ones of forked tongue
Have you no shame? She gossips
To fill the trees that's all been but emptied of its birds.
She speaks to someone
Other folks can't see

As she sheds all her clothes
In the dressing room,
She startles all too easily.
Suddenly what comes up for her?
The very reverend Mr. Eliot appears
As a full-fledged comely ghost in the glass.
She drops the mask and lets out a scream.
The days of romance are almost over
Once more rheumatism assails
Her hourglass figure once revered,
Was Mr. Eliot once her husband,
Or her brother to her sister's maid?
She doesn't know which way to go.
She calls forth spirits
In the dressing room
Until she can't anymore.

Prayers does no one any good.
All the street players have fled to the Crimean coast.
What was that she heard?
Her husband talking to her on the inner?
Was he not the one after telling her
No news is good news?

But then another voice interrupts her:
Woman prepare to meet thy god.
But this was not her time.
So she agrees to play hopscotch
And musical chairs
Until love merited an arrival
Or a hasty departure.
Some kind of academic accolade
In the offing, but for what?
Why wear a dress at all?
Why not accept the prize in dress pants?
A banquet is just a banquet,
And then it's over and then
You have to sleep
Alone and cradle the pillow of the Black Madonna.

The wrath of the poet's postal union half-forgotten,
When they went on strike last week
They forgot the increase in hourly wages
Won the year before.
Stamps of pristine herons,
Stars, bleak and out of date,
Their wings matted
With dreaded oil slicks.
Who forgets the oil spill spilling venom
Why hadn't the poison worked
What brought her to the verge of tears?

She thought of her brother
Crushed beneath a chassis of a car.
After that she couldn't bring herself
To work at anything. Even the thought
Of being a barmaid an impossible tryst,
Flawed in the wake of destiny's wake.
Could she help it, she was related
To the tsarina. A poultice applied
To her left ear failed to make anyone
Take any notice of what she said she heard.

All she knew the ravens' cries
Brought her to the brink of despair.
Acting or subtracting
The lid was off the id
We honor the elders by not talking
About such things as beset mother earth
As earthquake mudslides or lightning strikes
And yet we do not live in fear.

It's just we don't read the newspapers
And the telly had been on the blink for years.
Had we decided earlier to pull up stakes
On our encampment, we could have avoided
The new moon's spate of hungry sparks.
Such as it is, love is always hungry for itself
And the river bends one way to the north.
Until the last breath, we never could have believed
In irrigation's true portrait of sorrow.

Too Late My Brothers

It's a little late to make reparations.
I've burned my spinning wheel.
Your reply: what is done is done.
We've been used as women of comfort for such a long time.
Then when the tsunami comes, everyone yawns.
What about the old people still doing their knitting?
They live next to the reactors.
They don't want to move again and again.
Pele still has them by their shirt tails and their skirts.
Who watches for the soul news,
News that really matters does not matter.
What is it fails to shatter people's assumptions?
Who watches words fall out of both sides of mouths
Irrespective of *And Quiet Flows the Don*
Crops are failing and the drought continues.
What about the prisoners already let out of prison
What are they doing?
How can we cure inflation?
The indecision of grave robbers?
As a latch key child, I ask my mother:
O mother of mine,
Why was I left alone?
She answers:
Big girls don't cry. I don't.
Now she says
You're a mature women
You will survive.
I don't cheat on my taxes.
I only notice what is happening.

Squatting next to wicker baskets
In Spanish and Chinese laundries
Waiting for the high rises to rise,
While the hungry begin to grow more hungry,
Crop circles reinvent the medicine wheel.
The light that fled the mirrors of fair play
Is now given over to poverty's penury.
The sun's rays have no umbrella
To shield the face from truth.
Why is it every trapeze artiste dangles
In the great embrace and rapture of the Pleiades?
Keep your eyes on the grindstone.
Such a lovely string of pearls
To wrap around your neck.
Anyone who comes near my house,
I'll send them packing.
If they want my carcase,
They'd be much embarrassed
To find out how young
The havelina in my back yard.

Secrets

I told you all my secrets.
At least, I thought I did.
Carnal sin, the sin of indifference.
Imagine one dream I have not told you.
How can I be forgiven hymns,
Unpinned. yet still singing?
Built of bricks and mortar,
At best, each dream
Turned back from earth's
Sand-filled pitcher, hand poured.
If every act of kindness,
Held as an act of longing
For a harvest that simply
Refuses to exist, then
What am I doing? If in the wind
Of waking, I am still fed
By compassion's dance,
Tell me then of life's further
Circumstance, a slight melody,
The hidden life of cypress
And juniper, a shrill bird chirping
With an almost human eye.

Owl Woman

She wants to run back to Jamaica. Her lover left her. She has no one to run to. So what does she do? The tree branch outside the house, who does it belong to? Why shoot snowy owls?

She waited. She checked her engagement pad. She waited. Nothing happened. She wrote in her notebook. I foretold 2012. I foretold the tsunami. I foretold the coming and goings of my neighbors. Enlist the help of your spirit guides. Oh so do you come from New York too? You are accomplished as the waist on your oriental friend is wide. I took them all to the other side. Let's not add on years where they don't actually exist. I've drunken in all the sights and sounds that surround me until I am drunk on god. Don't you know I find it very difficult, oh so very hard, to exist in the world. Anyway, I hate to be co confidential with a friend I knew so long ago but I need to let you know while in this very body, you are already going back and forth to heaven. In my journal I recorded how the snowy owl came and went, the red-tailed hawk. On the deck a small sparrow hopped on my desk and would not let me go. He must have known I have so man y holy powers it hurts for me to tell you all about them. The awning that has always shielded me from the setting sun no longer does. Will the power of prayer protect me for yet another half a century. While away from here, I kept inside. It was very dark. The windows I sealed with brown bits of beaverboard board.

I kept myself to myself. I was in mourning for my brother, ,my father, my sister and my friend's sister and everyone who died. A book of common prayer declared after the birth of my eldest I should have been churched. But this was not to be. For I already knew who I was, I don't think anyone can see through me though. To most people I am a bit of opaque turquoise or jade. I don't want to parade my powers before the world. Giving a reading takes it out of me. I don't know how many breakdowns I've had. If I ever were a beautiful baby, just look at my dreads and wish you had such long hair as I have. All my friends call me every minute. My phone is ringing off the hook. Don't you know I couldn't tell you a lie. When I got back from Russia you told me throw all your holy medals away. You said after that it seemed so much darker in the house you could not even opened up the door or throw open the shades. Cripple Creek is where I lived for my knock down battle with sabbatical. Have you been to the salt baths? They say they will do you a world of good.

As for arthritis, I'm through with that. It's such a drag. Instead I remained churlish and out of reach. The dark forces overtook me. Everyone calls me on my phone. I'm half in and half out all the time Half here and half over there, if you know what I mean. Why can't I come clean and tell you everything I know? I've often asked myself the same thing. Thank god I don't have the guts to answer truthfully and to pull down my own set of questions. I'm burning with asides. I risk everything in my body just to bring the messages through. of course, you know you're a messenger too, I'm Jewish. I'm Indian. I'm Canadian from Sat. I'll be anything you want me to be. I'm bent out of shape by what I do and do not say. Tell no one what I've said. Why mimic the mocking bird casting down a crowd of black and white feathers? Why mirror the vagaries of weather? Why interpret the stealing of your purse as an act of God? Why tell of the lapses in consciousness when a poltergeist took over, the lights went out and everything went dark.

I'm out of breath. Until my last breath, I will occlude the vision of a thousand suns beckoning. Creationist sounds call me over. Over across the water until I can say I have truly found it. Found what I am looking for. A place to retire by the sea. Apparently then the power of prayer has not forsaken me after all.

High Rise

We saw a sign on the hotel. They said they wanted to attract new clientele like the twitterers and the googlers. These are in the new buildings and the old buildings. Some have exercise rooms, some have restaurants, some has this, some have that. But they are all purpose buildings like hotels for the workers to live in and have all their needs met. Day care centers etc. New jobs are being created. What happens to the homeless? Great screens are being erected outside the buildings on sidewalks where they used to sleep. The queues for people receiving goof from the Quakers stretches around three blocks. When the steam shovels came, the beds shook in which you slept.

You wondered how can an island support these buildings, what if the electrical grids fail? I recalled a strike in New York when there was no electricity.

My aunt May was alive then and it was difficult then but she only lived on the third floor.

Spirit Walk

I saw a woman at the street corner and she told me she saw five spirits balanced on a balance beam above the high rises. They were strong. I didn't understand what she meant. Then the woman disappeared. I didn't understand what she meant. I assumed she saw angels in the sky in the way I did not.

In the end, I wondered whether everything converged on the green potato bug. Since I had eaten worms in soup before and the insect was beautiful and I had heard of chocolate lavender ants. Nothing surprised me except that the bug had died. I felt sorry he had passed away. He was so beautiful.

From Whom All Secrets Are Hid

The last time it was reported
That we met, you were on a swing.
Later, when Granny threw us
A cold bit of meat upon a plate
Too late, we recognized
That cruel bit of Irish Stew. Too late.
At the time, we were not shown what to do.

That was then.
This is now.
I wanted to call
Our marriage quits.
No one had even thought
When to call the wedding banns,
A coverlet of white rose petals
Intertwined in a dream garden.
Not even a flute-player
Brought in from the coast,
Could interpret or boast,
With any fated sense of accuracy.
If anyone had thought to call
The wedding banns,
I don't recall who it was.
Perhaps, the priest
Was suddenly relieved of his duties.
Who was then the clown
That threw the gauntlet down?
Lest I forget, I always took the hit
For being a dinner guest out of sorts.

I recall what Granny came up with next:
Half-vexed, she stated Mother Theresa
Always counted her prayers
As events that could sweeten
The palette of forgiveness.
Later, you told Granny off:
But you know I am a vegetarian,
This morsel I may not eat.
Instead, just give me a bowl of rice.
Then you added in a sullen voice:
Mother Theresa, that was one hell
Of a woman,
A woman who had no choice.
From her beginning breath,
She knew which card to pick.
Actually, it was a war veteran
From the Isle of Mann who stated:
Before the gauntlet is thrown down
Know what it is you are rejecting.
Is there a certain tone of a voice by which
You expect to turn your life around?
Or will you elect to do the same thing
As you've always done:
Turn the other cheek and be done?
Or is there something else, nameless
More mysterious at work?
So, don't throw out the baby
With the bath, my friend.
Don't drown love in a silver tea cup
Poured by a disciple of truth.
Know the extent of a message
Sent from heaven, the breadth
And width and scent of jasmine
Enough perfumed incense

From a censer spilled
To set your soul on fire.
To keep you on the path, my dear.
For to and from you must come
One more time to be a disciple
Anything to get yourself from here to there
In short order. All the good it would have done
Your foot stayed against a stone
That might have tipped your soul right over.
Capsized your boat in short order.
In her last years, why did Mother Theresa
Lose her faith as easily as someone said she did?
You answered: mute swans are being killed this very day
To balance the so-called dance of nature.

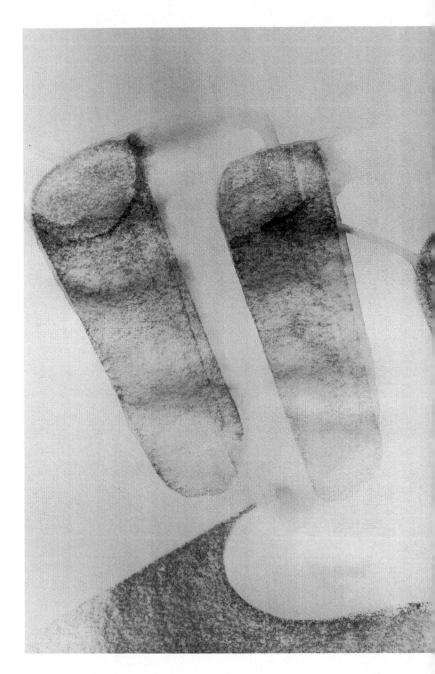

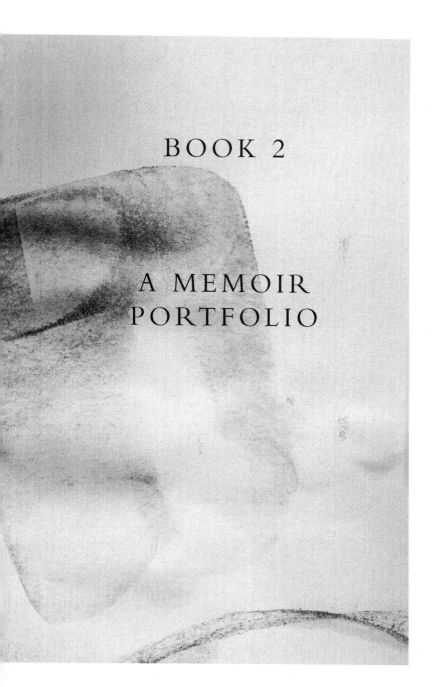

BOOK 2

A MEMOIR
PORTFOLIO

This is a fictional fantasy memoir.
Any relation to persons living or dead
is purely coincidental and synchronous.

Part I

Heart Song for a
Sometime Soul Brother

Change is good. How much could I endure without admitting the need for change? Change is frightening to some people. If change were frightening to me, I would not be around as a living, breathing representative of life on this planet. My entire life has been spent in the throes of anger over change. In fact, I've gone and endured so many changes, I have had to change my attitude towards anger and become peaceful. Instead, I have found cause to surrender to a "whatever happens" type of attitude.

Last week, for example, I was forced to change my room number in a given hotel over five times in one week. The fact, I don't own a house and instead rent property has caused me endless problems. Please, tell me, is there any easy way I can find some other kind of shelter? I feel I'm living inside the title of the Rolling Stones Lyric: *Gimme Shelter!*

I'm not sure which Rolling Stones album the song of my life most closely resembles. Contained within this universe of floating worlds, there's little rest left for the wicked. To this day, the meaning behind that mysterious proverb escapes me, does it you too? As much as I desire to make my invocations against the inevitable ravages of old age, whether envious of the future or not, sooner or later, I affirm the inevitable will take place. What I have ordered up for my life path includes being buried standing up.

Heavy-laden, I am out of breath from moving book-filled, blue suitcases from one room to another in the hotel. Don't get me wrong, I've always liked this hotel. No matter what time of day, it seems filled with a kind of subliminal, transcendent, and translucent, golden light that like fools' gold goes on shining and almost shimmering against the white-washed stucco walls. The white-washed walls even appear willing to reflect that kind of inner glorious light; no matter what few grey-edged reflections of uncertain and nebulous cloud cover would ever dare show up in this hotel room.

Am I in denial? Though an ugly green, like a long lost friend, the shag carpet surrenders to my mindful tread and greets my stubby and irritatingly solid toes. The texture of the woolen carpet make my toes feel as if I were a cat joyfully kneading her claws into flesh and purring with a bestial self- indulgence only poets can imagine.
Do I deserve to be human? Will I eventually stub my toe on the metal door sills comprising the door jambs in this hotel to confirm this fact?

I think I'm safe in this hotel. At least, that's what I tell myself. Today and tomorrow, things could change. I've never had a house and while idea excites me, I know I don't deserve a home. I am the only one that can get my body to do anything considered half-functional. A lot of adopted kids end up feeling the way I do. Inhabiting a body that is not worthy of being possessed and with absentee landlords who haven't a clue as to the powerful persona they wield from afar.

Each day in honor of possessing some kind of resistant strain of DNA, flesh, and skeletal frame, I have to perform a host of well-meaning and disciplined affirmations including one liners such as: Come on, body, you can do this! I know you're getting stronger! Come on! Come on! Get on with it! Prove to me you can do it! Otherwise, hurry up and give up the ghost forthwith. What's that? Don't answer me back! What's that you're telling me? You've just come onto me with the announcement you don't want to get up? It's seven o'clock. Tell me, you want to give everything up and start on another incarnation.

Too bad, body, would you like to admit defeat right now! You know the truth, I'm talking about. You're just kidding, right? Bone for bone, cell for cell, flesh for ungainly flesh, you will obey and do exactly what I say, right? You will not rebel. You will not start a revolution by defending your right to sit down at all times. You will get up. Being upright, you will begin to enjoy how the world looks. Have you forgotten about Gabriel García Márquez and how because of his writing, small towns have this personality absolutely no one can capture accurately? Everyone honors his persona, even cats and dogs and children have come to his grave to pay him court.

Meanwhile, on a more personal note, my body, yes, my body, you know the world abounds with stacks of pancakes and cream puffs awaiting your return to bestial bouts of indefatigable fatigue and hunger? One little trip to the corner deli and you won't even recall the degree of pain you recently experienced at seven o'clock in the morning. Instead, you will bow to the fact you are by now twenty pounds heavier after you have courteously digested that huge cream puff. You will savor the knowledge of instant debilitating degradation and thoughts that nourish your very existence. The roof of your mouth will feel like a swell temple in Bangkok or a cathedral in Montmartre. So delicious will be ingredients of that chocolate covered cream puff, will you will forget the word mouth the word pain as well as the word malaria. Sorry, if you need a tea strainer to figure this one out.

Yes, I know life is full of change. The persona of life as a hobo goddess presents as a transient reflection involving surrealistic multiple projections. Things will not always be this way. I look at old people and wonder: do you feel old? To myself, I think: do you know like them you look half-dead already. Do I really look that way too? Tinges of black and white streaks grace my otherwise auburn hair. No other sign of aging, though. People tell me, life will be such a blast in heaven! I hate to be doddering and old. I still feel the same way I did at seventeen. But the body does not feel the same way at all. It feels like a block of wood, it feels like an outlawed cigar box Indian that no one should ever have placed outside the boutique of old age.

That being said, once you have reached heaven, I am sure you can eat cream puffs all day and never get fat. However, one will probably have to anticipate murmuring or intoning an incantation consisting of a carefully worded steady stream of keening prayers. Such prayers are used to maintain the equanimity of the entire universe, the floating world so that citadels and palaces and pagodas made of glass and the real and unreal cathedrals won't ever leave the parameters of your inner heart-felt psyche. Thus, even in heaven you can eventually melt into the fragile sense of wonderment and ecstatic and never-ending bliss. As things stand now, body, I know you would be astonished to find yourself in the cathartic throes depicting the details attached to any kind of altered state. At least, not while you while away your life and continue dragging your heels over the flattened and previously fracking-filled wounds engendered by a very scarred and sorry Mother Earth.

Not unless you change, that is. Not unless you change or I change or someone somewhere in the world allows herself to change and the recalcitrant universe sets free all its captive and hidden pharaohs, aesops, and servants that might have at once unwittingly become enmeshed or underwriters in one of history's blessed and choreographed trajectories. I'm sure God hears all these monologues and intoned as entreaties similar to the following and then answers on his own account: Sister, sister, brother, please, please I've had all I can take. I've heard enough prayers for one day. So, please go get yourself to a convent and go seek out another angel to accompany through the trials of this life.

The angel you have borrowed is of a variety which is far too good for you. To my mind, my brother and god continues, though some your sentences on Mother Earth have been commuted, you remain continually undeserving of any blessing or sacerdotal accolades. Like god, my brother embodies some part of my history. I must always forgive and try to forget that sullen, unforgiving and none too penitent aspect embodied and embedded in the continuous displays of untold unmitigated displays of sibling rivalry.

Try the used car body dealership next time! OK! That's what my brother tells me from his secret grotto hidden behind his newly carved out grave stone. Turns out this particular grotto is really a used car lot, after all. He continues to inveigle the sympathy of anyone who will listen to him with a host of self-pitying and itinerant phrases.

Promise me you will trade in your angel for a new one. Besides, don't forget, he says, I newer model or one just like yours. They have put out lots of new lines of angelic power steering products this year. Just think about all the Buicks, Chevys, Audis and Pontiacs sitting detained behind the frozen glass of the showcase windows.

You remember the car grandpa had. Remember he gave it to me, not to you. It was because I was the only grandson. For him, I represented all his hopes and dreams. Come to think of it, a car would do you the world of good. No more dragging around town like a derelict woman. Your car named after several famous locations of Indian battles would probably appreciate it greatly if you purchased some shiny hubcaps and some wheels to keep her going in the morning.

With the possession of a new car body, my brother is firmly of the opinion I'd instantly feel a hundred years younger. I'm not sure I agree with him, but I want to let him know, with or without a car, I do appreciate certain styles of dancing. I do believe, though, that, contrary to popular belief, what is sauce for the goose is also sauce for the gander. Remember Ma used to tell us that. For instance, take the Cataline style of dancing. So popular was that style back there in the Seventies, kids in Youth Hostels all over the world took up this style of dancing. It was able to transform them and make change a viable option. I am all for change. That's why you need a new car body. Or at least a brand new car. But, my brother added, I am keeping a whole pile of money for you because as far as I am concerned you have been let loose from the local asylum and placed under recognizance only with my approval and my say so. I, alone, am the one in charge of your life, your personal mail, and your housing, not the government, but me, your homunculus, your homophobic brother.

Later, the Cataline style of dancing was replaced by salsa and tango. For a while, Youth Hostels and their minions ruled the roost. Everyone has forgotten the tenor of the good old days; today, some other kind of line dancing has taken over. But I digress. Wait, a minute, my brother has more to say. I know he's sometimes part of my pain but I love him so much, I cannot let him go.

Now my brother says: even in heaven, things go in and out of style rather rapidly. But, of course, I don't know much. I only got here last week. Never did get off that gurney. Hotter than hell in the local hospital corridor. Waiting around endlessly. The staff nurse and the interns, none of them would go out of their way to take you to the toilet when it was obvious you had wanted to go. Made me want to go to the can even more and so badly I wanted to call a hearse. Of course, then there was that part of me that didn't want to go. Didn't want to, but had to. Had enough of false alarms. Remembered how Dad finally went and I had nothing to do with it. I still don't have an ego. I was never a good dancer and I never got him the right car he really wanted.

When you first arrive in heaven, they give a kind of welcome home away from home celebration. Just like the people at local ice cream parlor; yes, though it's hard to believe because some places in heaven are hotter than others, they give you ice and cream and cookies. They call heaven the hospital so you won't suddenly freak out and realize you can't turn in the used car model for a last minute tune up, just one last time. Once you arrive in the heavenly hospital, you are in solitary confinement for life. Well, that's not really true either. You have to do a life review, and take a written exam to prove you will not try to run a railway crossing or a traffic light, and then you get some other examinations but I won't go into those because it might deter some people from trying to live a good life.

Want to let you know one detail about heavenly attire, most all the nurses have flying buttresses floating like wedding cakes on top of their heads; they also talk about Canadian geese a lot. You know, Sister, Dad did exactly the same thing I did. He went and had a good look around heaven and all, and then, true to his wayward style, he got cold feet and rushed back to life once last time just to make sure we could all hear him complain about the fact each of us wasn't taking good enough care of him. Now wanted a new bib. Now he wanted a new kind of Indian pudding smothered in plum brandy they can only legally serve to old people during Maori homecoming rites in some far flung corners of the British Isles. The fact is, as far as earth goes, Dad never did get enough dollops of his favorite coffee ice cream. I think that is one of the reasons he agreed to die. Too much attachment to the stuff of ego.

Yes, like I said change is always good. Especially, when it becomes imperative you need to let go of everything, especially the core essence of your ego. What I mean by letting go is to be able to willingly bid goodbye to of every last stick of antique furniture you thought you ever had in your back pocket.

Not as if anything but a comb and a billfold could ever fit in your back pocket. Every last chair you've ever sat in. Every last manner of lynx-eyed lunar eclipse you've ever dared stare at or gaze upon with binoculars for a long time until your eyes got crossed and your thumbs started to bleed. Eclipses can tell you everything about yourself until you actually end up swooning with the flames of a secret inner fire of self-knowledge. You know I could have become a top notch shaman or a minister, I don't know which; and it doesn't much matter. But it did matter a lot more did when I was out there walking on Mother Earth.

I hope Mother Moon does not take offense at what I say. Her blood-red eyes still reflect the russet strength of a hundred autumn leaves in a season of intense forgiveness. I am not sure which way forgiveness really travels. Is it Mother Moon is ashamed because of my heart felt and deep abiding love for her? Is it she who allowed me to walk on hot coals all her life while unreasonable almanacs spilled out the details of snowfalls, water levels, and man-made droughts and she shone that searching torchlight on my persona?

Mind you, I am not beneath allowing myself to choose to put the dog and cat out for a little romp in the woods. I know what you are thinking, sister, I often refused to take my dog for a walk because I was feeling so very blue and soporifically inclined and I often felt very sick after drinking myself half to death all night. I thought since I didn't have much time left over there on earth I would never want my dog to miss my talking her out for walks. No way could I prevent that from happening after my untimely and rather unseemly demise. Death is just like birth. No way to get around it. No way to get over it. Just like the song says. Yes, I admit it: In some ways I was actually already gone before I actually took flight. Dad was smart as a whip till the last minute. I was not so smart about the way I handled my life. I admit. I admit. I think I was absent not present for most of my adult life.

Dog died the week before I did. Meanwhile, since the lid is off the id right now, I will tell you this one thing: the inner workings of my heart and the god's truth. I know what I tell you feels right even if it is wrong. The fact is, God and you both know that my dog and I were very tight.

We had the most fantastic relationship that anyone could ever likely maintain and entertain while on earth. Dog told me she told me she would kick the bucket one week before I did. Course, I didn't believe a word she said. She'd been with me longer than Mom and Dad ever admitted. I always hid my feelings from them. Ever since I can remember, they told me I didn't deserve a puppy because I didn't know how to take care of myself. Like I told them, they never should have sent me to that fancy boarding school.

I didn't have a born again boarding school hairdresser the way everyone else who attended that school did. They were fashionable and very bourgeois people. There was no way I could measure up. The stakes were too high. Maybe it was that road rage accident Ma had with the dump truck while I was still tucked so safely away in her womb that changed everything in my life. I don't know but trauma like that scares the Bejesus out of you for your entire life. Mother and child both. Perhaps, that is why she loved me so much, much more than the other children she might have wished she'd rather not have had.

You know, today, science has the inborn capacity to explain every detail or every single mood swing you've ever experienced during the course of your life. I think I was more of an Indian or a country style preacher than I'd like to admit. I had this wary kind of ethics about me. I hate to admit I used to embarrass both my birth parents by looking at the motion of the ocean's waves and dreaming far too often.

While on earth, I also had this irritating habit of drawing myself back into myself. Don't get me wrong, I still fear the power of the Lord once in a while. This surprising because, without a body, I have no real sense of maintaining any kind of control over my environment. Because in the same way of the wary eye of the moon that glorifies all Beings down on earth, I do believe the Lord has a really magnificent grip on some kind of practical and caring kind of reality.

Blood-shot red eyes. Mine were all bloodshot that day. I had been drinking day and night for a week trying to get up courage to do it. I have always had the courage. I think that's what allowed people to nourish the tendency to get up and to then dishonor me so much. They didn't have the courage to tell me the truth. I alone had the courage to tell myself the truth. End it all and at least have some measure of decency and control over the narrow corridors of my life. Though I haven't caught sight of him yet, I still believe Dad would approve of what I did. He didn't believe in the Lord and because he didn't, he was the one who gave me the strength and sharpened my thoughts to where I could follow through with my vision and surrender my inborn sense of agnosticism and atheism.

A miracle when I got to heaven! I found I could still reason like a trooper that without ever going to the church of grammar to get wind of some phony kind of a trumped up religion. That was such a relief. Like the ethics of the Midwest, heaven seemed real. I can't stand it when certain gospel preachers preach some like some kind of weird robotic plan that includes the idea you gotta believe in something, you gotta have faith, you just have to do something proper and fitting instead of sit around all day and get drunker than a loon or a coot on a country lake.

Even for all my training in the military, I didn't even have a clue as to how to take proper aim. Despite all, that I did achieve a proper aim, you know what I mean? But I told you I always knew I had the proper means, the proper way to go out and one day I would actually accomplish what I set to do. I would not be a failure all my life. Yes, like I say, change is good. I admit I sometimes go into the depths of crying out for the Lord in the same way I used to do on earth, but I am different now.

Though it may sound strange to say it, I am more grounded in heaven than I was on earth.

That memorable day when I took the girlfriend to look at the beautiful green and blue waves, I wished I had asked her then. But I could not bring myself to do that. I was too young and she was much too old to ask of her. I mean anything so deep and so loving that expressed the way I felt. In this regard, it seemed I lacked courage and even if I would pin a barrette or a brooch on her person today, I would not hesitate to say the words. I would not hesitate to tell her: I want you to know right now at this very moment, I love you so. Right now, I want to tell her I went and slept all day the birthday card she gave me in March. Like a sacrament, the card appeared to lie undisturbed for centuries. Its approximate location beneath my head where it was hidden beneath my goose down pillow every night gave me a strange sense of support and security.

I recall the day of gift-giving and the upturned mischievous little smile of hers planted firmly on her mouth. I remember how Dad was acutely furious at the card and the gift-giving ceremony. How he sputtered into the angel cake and recited a host of indignities to the effect: how utterly atrocious! Really, I don't expect such actions from hired hands! He was astonished by the fact my secret girlfriend so freely handed that beautiful birthday card around for everyone to look over during my birthday celebration. From the first, when I played her that Tom Rush Song, you must understand, it wasn't for you my sister; I know that's what you thought at the time. Of course, I forgive you for that little indiscretion of yours so typical of your inborn romantic nature. But, no, the music I played on the car stereo, it was all for her! Such was the depth of my heart ache. I still feel that ache in my heart all the way over here in heaven.

Like I told you earlier, change is always good. I loved her from the beginning of time and had she been over one hundred years old, I would have still loved her with the same intensity accompanied by a sudden dash of almost shameful honor and that inveterate sense of shyness I have suffered from all my life.

Part II

Letter to my Guatemalan Daughter

Something niggles, something bothers. Something does not set right with me. Some writing is careless. Some letters are belabored and scripted secretly in lemon ink. Something is very unnatural. Something is not right. Pomeranian princes are not a dime a dozen. This is not an adoption. Adoption is not a loving option here. It is just a good old-fashioned lie to save the truth from reaching the garish multitudes who want to know: did you slee with a black man or did you not? Guilty as charged. I can't hide it from the masses, nor could I hide it from you.

Why it is you don't you want to meet your father? He says he will bring his sacred violin to you in Albuquerque. However, he never shows up. Later, he says, maybe later he will show up. True to form, he never showed up for the wedding, either. But I was taken in. I believed he would attend my wedding. He said yes, yes, yes, of course there will be a wedding. But, he is lying. Unbeknownst to me, there simply won't be a wedding, after all. Surprise, surprise! Perhaps, I am hard of hearing after all. Mostly, I feared what I feared most had occurred. Mostly the words I heard were: the wedding will not take place.

Despite my presumption of innocence and despite the thickness embedded in the matted knots in your nappy hair, your father never cared enough to put his name on the birth certificate and marry the woman he had definitely knocked up. It is as simple as that. That is the truth. Some men are like that. I was innocent enough. My mother never told me anything about it. I had to figure every detail of my life out for myself. I was a throw away child. Given no sex education whatsoever. You have never been a throwaway child. You were the opposite and much too important.

You ask about a birth certificate. In this world of yours, there are no birth certificates. It seems officials ran out of ink. You wish to avoid poverty in this life. No one blames you for that. What is it that I cannot understand about your life? If I catch any hint of anything resembling a sleep pattern or hold up my hand against the Rorschach shadows of the midnight sky, why do I cry when the truth is the truth and you did not die.

At night, stars shine brightly and I am not there to behold any proof of the light of the world reflecting the sheen and patina of those dancing divas. There it is. Now tell me what is love? The skirt of love? The blouse of love? A hairpin detour? A turn, a change of heart? Tina Turner's fantasy? The kindness of an embrace comprised of filigree stars that are faceless and obsolete in Italian paintings that lack the perspective of vanishing points. Why do people write letters to one another? Using all the letters of the alphabet will not make any difference as to the outcome in my life. Only time embraces absence still there is no sign of any kinship among any of the Pleiadian entities that comprise our bodies.

Here's what it is. Here is what this story is all about. I can't forget what you said to me the last time we agreed to meet and you intimated to me you used to think I was once your mother but now you stated that I would never be that person again. You cannot unhook motherhood from the eyeholes of time and bear witness to a travesty of a wayward goddess. Regarding this issue and Athena being born from the head of Zeus, do you know what Yogananda says?

He declares the mother is closer to the children than the father, but for you to deny the reality of both, I wonder do you want to be in this world, at all. To my mind, such a thought would result truly in be insanity, my friend. You've announced you'd never be poor. The ghost of poverty would never knock out the hollow innards of your door. If I remained poor, you would never speak to me again. Did I have a choice? I had to find work wherever I did, whenever I could. Why is it I think of the glittering stars as diadem-infested statements of wealth, the wealth of the universe, and the wealth of the myriad of the jewels you wear so freely and no ever questions asked?

All jewels stolen from me in recollections of something resembling non-tranquility and impressions of immortal lies. When I agree to lie down in green pastures, what being will accompany there. When I die, will I commit to think of Navajo sheep? I am a follower of what happened to all of those tribal lands. Lands that have been stolen like the goats, the horses, as well as all the nameless glittering jewels you wear. I think of all of Chief Joseph's colorful raiment. I think of that singular Biblical passage that addresses supper for the birds. It is not a text or a subtext such as Supper for the Birds and yet it is all part of the same woven subtext and cloth.

What about issues allowing that birds of the air and lilies of the field must remain in untilled fields as we humans admit trials of the flesh for which we constantly toil and spin? My dear, we cannot forget these innocent winged drops of blood that we see flying about us. Nor can me forget the mute swans, the trumpeter swans, and swans that stay on the ground because they fear to fly.

Do you know how many drops of blood some birds have within their tiny feathered frames? If you have seen one of them fallen stunned or dead on the snow, you will know the answer to this question. Whoever has agreed to live on earth with us, who are they, and what are their assignments? We need the bird relatives to steer us on the right path. We need the animals to graze the fields. We need the fields. Now add words for fields and for animals. Don't shy away from the task at hand. Don't shy away from the truth, my daughter.

Dignity? Reverence? Honor? We have our dignity. We have our

morals, our morality, our proverbs, our ethics. Without these, would we not inhabit the world as mere court jesters or tricksters of the wind? If we remain truly lonely for our souls, then would we not be remiss to demand such a prenatal and penitential arrogance. Instead, we swim as arrogant conquistadores and make no mention of the dreadful happenings that have occurred on Mother Earth. So we remain somewhat innocent, arrogant, and unknowing as to the identity of the ravens who till the fields of our imagination and leave us gasping for breath.

Coming from a daughter with a mother like me, my words may serve as your music. Unspeakable, Unthinkable. A revenge for my not having acceded to the projected image of the garden party. If the queen,being who she is and who she was, before she died, were the one who failed to be amused by your words, then what about me? Am I not amazed, astonished by your total lack of compassion?

Well I really don't know how you have turned out. Whether you really care for the indigent, the poorly sick, the needy, and the elderly. And the blameless, whoever they are. The poor live in the knowledge of lack they have no voice and have no choice. They know lack. They live in hovels. They are living in this, not a third world country, and yet in some ways, a third world country of ignorance, lies, and deception. What country is this they dwell in? Would you even admit, they live, they dwell, and they make their mean and cantankerous beds in a country of suffragettes, in a country of self-satisfied, smug placard-waving hordes? Through no fault of their own, the poor are truly poor.

Well, as a young person, I knew from the get go where such a smug and devil-well-may care-sorry-attitude would take me. Not very far. That's what you thought I said. Perhaps that's what you believed. I assure you, down the road of health; such an attitude would put me in the aggrieved state of mind. A state of mind, I allow that is somewhat similar to that of a hospital intern already ministering to those who cannot escape the cramped confines of the almshouse, the poor houses. What about the wretched, the old charity cases? Old age is surely then but a virus of those that are forever poverty-stricken. What kind of a blasphemous type of evening news is this falling from the lips of my own daughter? What kind of a lip gloss is this? Look how she glibly and arrogantly she glosses over more than half of century of humanity's fevered, rancid, and despicable rabble, all rabble before her dark eyes. She assures herself she will never be one of these? She assures me she wants to forget and erase her entire childhood. She wants to forget the rez. The real people of community.

The air conditioner that didn't exist. Jewels that were stolen as soon as she was born then given back to her. The Kinaaldá ceremony she refused to have performed on her behalf. The neurologist's reports that stated when she had an accident she was truly hurt, badly hurt. The trauma, the wound. A soccer ball that was kicked by a classmate. The fact of the soccer ball never happened? Where it came from? Where she came from. Didn't want to recall. The heat going off, the pipes bursting. In the trailer that nurtured her and set her down. Quietly upon the stage of life. Wouldn't stand for being any bit of reality resembling the penny-pinching poor.

Poverty's best friend certainly not yours. You have made the wrong decision, mother. You have witnessed my being born on the wrong side of the tracks. Yet you track in mud from a trackless universe that has no country of borders, no boundaries and no words to assist the healing of the masses.

To let down the hem of a favorite dress. It was like saying. God dammit! I promise you I will never wear a green dress without a gardenia. Painted on the strap. Printed on it or sewn on the breast. It was your icon, your medallion, a medal for your war pony. After declaring the war on poverty. What else was there left to sing about? To write home about. Hob-nobbing with friends. Playing poker and billiards, after all that smugness was not intended to be your best friend. Oh come on now. Your ego defenses are like fallen feathers on the wind of song. Bear witness to this unguessed dream of yours.

What better world is there than the world of metaphor, an escape from the world of desperation in which you play your violin?

Part III

The People In and Out of the Picture

I have chosen a picture of childhood when I was caught within a visual lens while balancing on the rather slender railing of a fence at the local beach club. I guess it was a club but I never joined it. I wish I possessed a balance beam and make such a thing work on my behalf. Did not want to fall.

I regret what happened after the picture was taken. Seconds later, I fell and bruised my public bone very badly. At seven I was very serious. I told no one what had happened. Accidents were just a part of life. According to my mother, the human body was indestructible. I didn't know what a pubic bone was. Or that the body was. Or, what it was. I just knew I wanted to dance and be like an elf, a ghost, or a spirit trapped in the story of *Les Sylphides*.

My mother commented she thought was reliving a past life as a trapeze artist. That's what she said when she saw this picture. I was hoping that wasn't true because of the fact I remembering falling and ending my life that way before. But I don't really believe in previous lives. I think we are experiencing all of them now, all at once.

While the picture has come to symbolize my cutting edge style of poetry, (that is really not that cutting edge at all), I don't really like the photo all that much. In the picture, I think I look too stupid for words and someone who probably destined for immediate failure of some kind.

I still feel that way. Nothing has changed in my attitude towards the self. All this talk of loving yourself. It doesn't work when you are set out to pasture too young. You have to be very stubborn to survive. You have to take care to not care about a lot of things. For, if you cared, you would dissolve in wreaths of writhing self-pity and self-contempt that Edgar wrote about.

There is no way I would understand the concept: self-care and all the attractive words that define the divine feminine and the nurturing of the adolescent body. In my day, women were women and what happened next just happened. No one complained. No one was vexed or annoyed. You just buried the hatchet and said kind words about everything. No one suffered trauma. No one knew what crisis was. Everything was part of nature. Life was a series of unquestionable happenings as a woman you just took in your stride.

Meanwhile, I have to like the fact I took the challenge in the photo of assuming a defiant posture. I tried to make my persona look self-assured, confident, and physically fit. Meanwhile, this balancing act would later presage the possible tendency towards the gratuitous nature of failure.

No one should have such a childlike and frail ego as I knew I had and then survive. What did I know about trying to be a kid? To act so poised, I was bound to fall. To a find out a way to balance and keep going whether I knew I was going to fall or not, how could I ever do that? I didn't like the fact my mother knew who I was. As an artist, she was critical of me from the day I was born. Yet, I do see the photo reflects a determined little tadpole, one who is hell bent on keeping the discipline of the spirit path wherever it might lead.

Later, in life my mother told me I was one who should never have possessed any firm idea of where I was going. She questioned my interest in metaphysics and ballet. Both interests she declared were dangerous and bad for the health and happiness of small children. Of course, meanwhile, my mother wanted to be an actress. But she never went into the fact my father banned her from the stage; yet, each of her three children got bitten by the stage struck bug creatures anyway.

I chose this picture because it reflects a time before I was fostered out and had to leave all that was semi-secure and somewhat familiar behind. I chose the picture because it gives the illusion of strength. I can still remember the seersucker shorts and how I felt that day. I felt I had to initiate this challenge even though it seems totally impossible. My body was hot and I thought by climbing up on a high thin railing, I could enjoy a light breeze. Instead, on top of the railing, I noticed the wind was still as rainwater in a barrel.

The day the picture was taken, it was certainly very hot; the rose bushes lining the beach were rank with the perfume of over 80 degree fahrenheit weather. I wanted to be tall. I wanted to be noticed. I think my grandfather always encouraged me to stand up there and do something. He had a way of demanding the highest and the best from me. Then he would always document everything by taking a perfect shot of what was rather an imperfect situation.

From looking at the picture, I think my arms look very long and floppy and are not even formed properly. I felt my body was not really shaped in a way that would serve me well. I always felt bow-legged.

One of my arms looks longer than the other and seems definitely not as determined as the other. Then too, my legs appear rather stubby and useless. If I could go back in time, I would not have tried so hard. I would have sat back in a deck chair and enjoyed the view of the waves but that may be due to my rather escapist and aged contemporary perspective.

As to the figures that encouraged me to act a certain way and wanted to shape and sculpt my future they are now all deceased. I feel rather miffed at my grandfather for while he encouraged me as a young child to be a certain way, he later changed. When I got older, he began controlling me too much. He wrote a letter to my parents which I later found many years later.

It seemed truly a terrible letter for he spilled the beans behind my back. He was angry at my parents for having sent me away from home at such a young age. He told them that I was wasting away, was in ill health, and was suffering from dangerous bouts of anorexia. Of course he was right. He was always right.

That's because he was Indian; Indians are always right. Grandfather didn't discuss with me the contents of the letter he'd sent to my parents at all. The letter sparked a familial crisis because my parents never wanted me to come back home whether I failed at my dancing classes or not. But grandfather wanted me to go straight back home. He threw me out of his apartment because his wife found us together in his bedroom. That was enough to make anyone unsure of puberty rites feel somewhat promptly rejected.

So in my memoir, this letter serves as the keynote speech for ultimate betrayal. I thought think my grandfather was incapable of doing anything wrong. Across the wide divide of heaven, I still love my grandfather to this day. Meanwhile, the day I read his letter, I felt the double jeopardy of intimate betrayal. I'm sure my grandmother did too. But maybe she was relieved what happened, happened. But she never left his side. No matter what, she didn't.
We never spoke together about what happened as a bit of a jarring incident or a non-happening. Things happened you never spoke about. I just wanted a home with loving parents or grandparents, it didn't matter who the people were as long as there was love involved, a love you could feel like the caress of rainwater on your back.

After what happened, I was thrown back in the boarding house again. Later on in my life, I knew I would travel far away from all the madness of rejection. I did travel far away but, in my travels, I never did really seek out nor did I discover a loving family. Nor could I ever figure out what I did wrong that rendered my parents so unwilling to keep me at home. It seemed there was some reason they wanted me to disappear too much. Today, I figure they wanted my money. Yesterday, I figured they wanted my body. Tomorrow, perhaps I may come up with another explanation. I have no final reflection. No final answer. I didn't need to be in foster families. They had the money to care for me but they hadn't the interest in being good parents.

My newer explanation is that there was an affair between my mother and someone else, and also my father and someone else. I was the product of that someone else. I don't know what exactly happened. Maybe one day I will find out. So far, I haven't. So, my life is composed of this great big question mark. I never asked to be a writer. I never asked for the talent I have. But it has been a burden because even though a memoir is supposed to be the recollection of truth (even if it is recollected in tranquility), I don't know what the truth is so I feel like a failure as a memoirist.

The other thing that happened in my life is that my ballet teachers were split over my future. Two thought I should make a career and two thought not. But my grandfather and parents lied to me and said none of the teachers thought I could make a go of it. When a child is lied to, it makes for bad blood and a severe lack of trust.

I decided I needed to do something with the picture. Perhaps put to bed the memories surrounding its being taken in the first place. So I had it blown full size into a six foot portrait and took it to the fair. I put it up next to my booth at the fair I attended.

I thought the picture would tower over my slightly hunched over seventy year old frame. Instead, when I looked at the picture, I never thought the poem that with it went with it did the picture any kind of justice. I felt my vulnerability and my conditioning about the picture was too strong. Instead, of this picture I wanted to behold a picture of a girl with long flowing hair and a long flowing gown running through a field shouting I am free, free at last.

Part IV

Midwife to the Goddess of Water

The wind soft on my shoulders. The soft, afternoon wind. The sun. The sun warming the entire world. A word of gratitude. Where is this place? It is a country estate. It is a bathroom painted blue by a workman from long ago. The place of the afternoon bath, calling forth a room large enough to be placed inside any dream picture of what needs be the central place for a large enameled bath tub. Bath tubs can be filled with geraniums and be antique fixtures to create art projects. Or bath tubs can remain in splendid isolation. A Renoir painting of the afternoon bath. That's what I had in my mind. My mother bears resemblance to the women in Renoir's paintings.

She wants all her children to be artists. To look at children as part of the furniture as if the children inhabit a sacred sanctuary where only artists can encompass and inhabit spheres of creativity. And this they cannot quite do fully enough. Yet, there is something inhumane and inappropriate about all of this.

Here is picture of what was. The shudders on the window thrown open wide. A slanted meadow so welcoming with its vast array of dandelions, dandelion fluff, and compasses that clock the profusion of growth on the farm: wild flowers and plenty of thistles that would scrape your hands if you leaned down to pluck a scotch broom or a thistle flower.

My hands drenched in lukewarm bath water. The reflection of the blue painted walls. The water blue, blue like the lap of the ocean. The cup of blueness. The blueness of a sky that has never seen any hint of cloud-filled rainstorms.

My daughter, Tiara, paddling and making the unhurried noises of a child having all the time in the world moored in the bright blue birthing water in the life span of an afternoon. I'm a little brown duck sitting in the water. Her body covered in water, feathered and warm. Her brown hair matted with a distinct dalliance of one who can converse with water spirits.

The water surrounding her, pure, her skin shining and warm with the warmth of new shining pearls, undiscovered and harbored in warm gentle waters that gentle her too as in an embrace of sacred mentoring that will keep her safe and secure. The life of a child? The life of a pearl. Who dives for the pearls and sings for his supper in an opera called The Pearl Fishers?

Have you ever descended deep enough into the welcoming depths of ocean, deep enough to catch sight of a pearl through the cleaving walls of blue oyster shells bedded down?   In a perfect orchid of clusters. Like a cluster of grapes. Ovaries. An undercurrent of the world never made up but always a fact. I mean those blue, transparent jewels perfumed with the lisping consciousness and clear blue syllables of water far too deep to defend any sense of stillness. Pearl eyes. Water spirits. Glass eyes. A silence too clear and too pure for the lips of sound to whisper past or through the
walls of sound.
Caribbean pearls? You cannot find them just anywhere. They have existed long before time began and time ended. For centuries. Pearls cleave to the throat of empresses. You dare not feast on the antics of youth. You do not see the pearl-fishers every day trying and vying for luck. For the knuckles of waters can swallow everything alive and make no mention of anyone willing to risk everything in sacred acts of survival and surrender.

Pearls. A pearl tiara. Her eyes swift, darting, and brown. My eyes on her. That water now courting her soul a second time since the time of her birthing underwater. A Leboyer birth. The clock on the wall tracking and ticking the beginning days since the shaped birthing of her petite karma, a karma that will never be over until the day is young within the easy bell-chiming time taking all the time in the world to effect the gospel of birth in the childhood weather of water.

The afterbirth. The placenta. Drowning in the palace of love. Whence cometh the child that can sit in the palm of your hand? The painted blue clapboard timbers of the bathroom wall, a wall whose paint now chipped with blue painted tears peeling from the soundless space of the solace of a walled in space. Solace. Eye-sockets of water. Blue water falling from the hinges in the dreaming spaces of a dream that is never quite done, never quite over. Birds flying over water. Water. The unhurried spoken truth of water. Spools of water rewound. Spokes of water, carefully worded, carefully woven, reworked, revoked, turned, returned to wheel and then revealed as inner and outer speech of mendicants.

The speech of mendicants rewoven in threadbare clothes, revoked, rescinded, words given and taken and then reworked and reworded; words finally revealed. Biblical words. Proverbs that take up the slack of the universe when it wanders off track. Hath the rain a father? A mother? A mother of all feathers? Is that not enough to give your child sup? Unhurried, shirred, stirring lips of water moving and unmoving. Innocent words of a child, a mother. God speaking to the innocents abroad.

My paean, my ode, my poem, my song to the unhurried sound of water. The water absurdly peaceful, water hung with a tapestry of sound, water absurd, so blue, yet blameless, the feast of words waiting to give nourishment to the lonely and dispossessed? We know what you have done. Do we know? We know what the spirits have said. We know what has been done. What time has accomplished. It has wrinkled the blue lips of water. The wrinkled lips of time are divine. No thought is ever completed. No life is ever completed. That is why we keep coming back. Yet nothing is ever fully completed on the page.

Is not the world full of sorrow? Enough sorrow to mend the idle palaver of sparrows, purveyors and messengers of time's timeless wounds, gaping and unafraid? The meanest words lie undisturbed upon the page before the listening ear. Where are the listening ears? Are we all asleep? Can we wake up long enough to yawn, to make mention of our unease at being in the world?

Water is the memory of birds, of bird-like hands. Water is a blue heron ruffling its own feathers, such deliberate feathers, half- owned that never bothered to shape anything but that which it wants to own but cannot own. So when in a sacerdotal reverie you recall after all you are her mother, when you dip your hands into water, you greet the world, you learn the hard way what you've come to know.

A duck purring in the water. The thirst I have for memory whispering in my ears. Compassion's thirst, never quite over. Her hands purring in the runnels of blue water as if time could never stop its spate of blathering moments. Honoring her now and her child and her child's children. Time somehow talking up a storm of a sudden.

Time's hem and lens of memory taken up and let down again. But I swear, child, I don't remember a thing of what I've said. Call in a tailor from the import export house and drowsy, he will know how to take up the hem of sleep for those that wonder whether the garment of speech will fit in the wonderment of the bewildered soul.

If time were a wishing well, I would throw bright coins over my shoulder and make a wish that time would come back and once more throw up her form up upon the shore of remembering and time's indifferent offering of remembrance. The clock ticks. If water could talk back.

Almost in the way of beginning to be able to tell you telling you, telling me the beginning and the end of a half-forgotten rime: Put your hand in the hand of the man who never was one to talk back. So why is he talking back now? Adjusting his hat? Just like that. Apologize? For what? I never. You never. The shallows of the water interrupt the ruptures in time's memory map of the whole world. What's the man doing in the picture? Doesn't he know enough to know he does and does not belong?

Whose voice is the one I hear? Is this the voice of Pan? If so, the voice of Pan is never sated, never stops It seems he is the one who shapes the fated taking back of humming birds' wings and loosens the stem of longing and the tongue of honey- suckle in summer vines that water within the crimped shallows of a summer afternoon.

Water has a conversation with itself. That's why we're gathered in a dialogue here in this space. here. In this place. At this time. We still would swear, each one of us, help me with this; water never talks back but holds her skirts in place, smoothing down the wrinkles of time like this. Like that. Put your hand in the hand of the man of the man who knows how to walk on water.

Whenever he likes to recall a coveted season of remembrance. He talks back like the clock on the wall that swallows occasions of celebration disappointment anticipation, and elation. You hear the water. You hear the clock on the wall. You touch your daughter's little hand. You sing to her with the voice of a wren or a sparrow coming of a sudden upon the precarious landing of a tree branch that is never ending.

Will it be you find or take comfort in memory's birds? The apple tree in the meadow sings of the mantra: Let no harm come to anyone. Take comfort in that. Stroke her face. Her hair. Water rising to the top of memory's ragged branches. What could have saved her from memory's avalanche of minutes? In the trading post of minutes we all know what time means. Uncles and aunties, all gather round. Witness the ancestral would of time's healing. In the surround of the big picture, time knows no wound. No fabric. No silk tapestry of birds whose blurred bodies sink into the cloth. Want not, waste not.

I recall the night she was born. I was sitting in am embroidering class. Mao Khang, a Hmong friend and midwife told me what time it was. The time of the child coming. Such a time. Baby is coming, she said: Are you sure? How do you know? Mao said. We know such things. I know such things. See, just look at the shape of your breath. Like the frost rising from sun warmed snow. Look at your breath see the smoke circling, rising and falling from the great mountain granary of sleep.

Look at the curve of your breast and your belly. Look at the child reeling from the touch of the welter of water within. Inside the door of sound. She waits. Walled in by my water's sweet sense of reckoning. Water welling up and keening. Look how you're always out of breath. One last desperate gasp of breath and then she will be born. You only have to walk from here to there across the wooden floor of death and the life that's in your breath to see her, to hear her, to feel her waiting to be born.

She wants to stretch out her wings on earth and she's tired of pretending to be patiently waiting, all the while, waiting as an angel child. Aching to be born. Is it not in my daughter's innate manner of awakening to resilience she must show forth her light to the world? For she is yet desperate for someone to show some sign of affection for the valley of shadows in a shadow-filled birthing room. You know not everyone makes it into the world.

You can't argue with nature and all her distinguished relatives. You can't figure on nature looking the wrong way round in the way of seasons, in the way humans can when they lose touch with circadian cycles between sleep and waking. A moth does not fly to the wrong star to be born. A Luna moth can incarnate in as little as one week.

Otherwise, why leave behind the elfin masked presence fetus womb-tomb cocoon behind? So much for plant digestion and all the leaves of plant medicine she has eaten before she shows the world how much she is so dying to be reborn. Do you think a sparrow beginning to map a magpie's flight would ever be grateful to fall from a tree out of reach of memory' ken.

A sparrow never falls short of breath. Think again on this, daughter. Think again. The midwife, Mao Khang, steps back in time. Something makes her stop in her tracks. Sits back on her heels. Steps back from the blue, shuddering wave of eternity to tell you this. To tell me this. Mao Khang takes me by the hand. We walk up the steps. We walk into the chapel of the birthing room. That my hand does not slip out of hers. I hope that I don't make any missteps. This is my first time. How well she knows it. This is my eldest. She knows it. Water talks back. Water tests the unlearned and lessons of time. Love life, love time. Love life, my precious one, for this is my first time, this is your first time.

Part V

Portrait of My Mother and Me

That God is usually totally unavailable for comment. This may come as a shock to many people. Don't you believe me? I am my mother's daughter. That makes me a credible witness to the illegitimate tales she recounted me during the course of my youth. People who are conversant with the wind, what do they know? People who are god-fearing, church-going sun-worshippers or avid consumers of the greater human good embodied in little stucco-filled statues of Mother Mary imported from Medjugorje, would they have believed my mother as I did? I was a defenseless little sheep. Innocent. Not a victim, exactly. But I was a maiden shaped by indecent bouts of sincerity, duty, and, above all, a sense of loyalty

Somehow had I been my neighbor's daughter, I might not have fallen between the cracks in the sidewalk. This I did as a child while remaining truly obedient to the meditation my mother projected on my delicate frame that usually sported pink frilly dresses and black patent leather shoes.

Such dress shoes were meant only to be worn in God's Sunday school's dancing classes. In a freeze frame, I can still see myself wearing the pink dress adorned with a baroque variety extra red smocking encrusted across the non-existent bosom.

Don't believe a word of what I say, my mother intoned, but one day I would not be surprised that you might find yourself abandoned and left for dead on the side of the road like that bag lady. Then she gesticulated with her long fingers towards non-existent people. Perhaps she saw ghosts as I did. It was all part of her scenery. Make sure you think story this over. To me, her words meant I would be confined to the corner of an attic room without recourse to the open windows always cloistered and cosseted from the out of doors and fresh air. To me her words coasted over my frail form like spring rain but I didn't take into account what her words would do to me later on in life. The life of a child is surly and sullen, yet from one day to another, moods vary like the amount of rainfall and nothing is considered an impossible truth.

Remember your Aunt Romana and what happened to her. Immediately, upon your uncle's death, she threw herself inside an eiderdown and she was not heard from for two years until the undertaker's took her out as if she were one of a cotillion of ants on a run to a bakery full of crumbs. That Aunt Romana's life was cut short due to an abandonment of god and the angels did not stop the demand for my top ranked performances tap dance routines that entertained the veiled and well- heeled ladies who were constant attendees at the ice cream socials at the Lady's Auxiliary at the Darby and Joan Club. God will punish you if you don't use your talent, my darling girl, my mother told me.

This made me aspire towards the untrammeled heights of the higher fountains of heaven's largesse which would shower upon my head some kind of future. A future that might include not only a communion veil but perhaps a matrimonial veil as well as perhaps even a postulant's veil. This would only occur if I decided to profess. To profess was like a story of a condemned woman who was stoned to death because she did not take her mother's words seriously enough. The other side of heaven contained all the contents sequestered within the dark corners of Mr. Capezio's Gypsy and Hammered Nail Boutique.

What greater torment and disappointment than to have to enforce a predisposition towards visiting Mr. Capezio's Boutique week after week. The man suffered many curses because he kept the prices at a level ill-afforded by anyone who refused to pay on time.

Carol Cardozo's family insisted that each of their nine children had merited a scholarship for tap dancing shoes that extended for the next fifty years. But my mother washed pots and pans at the local restaurant. God had punished me with bearing witness to this incredible set of luggage I would carry for most of my adult life.

Yet, unlike Cardozo's family, my mother and I had to return to Capezio's each week for three years in order to replace the metal tappers that got worn out with every routine. My mother said it was because she knew how to play the violin like the devil that I was honored with a few pennies every weekend. She explained that the ladies felt sorry that my communion dress had bullet holes and cigarette stains on the lace collar and that this was the only way to the heavenly gates other than exile from the old country.

My mother also explained to me that if you played the violin too well God would punish you for that too because only Jesus and St. Raphael knew the width of talent that was no bigger than the tiny tree trunk branches that comprised my wrists and ankles that might snap at any moment and end my fledgling career. Before such accoutrements were ever in style, my mother insisted I would wear tender little ankle bracelets graced and adorned with circles of miniature heart-shaped or fish-shaped charms and tiny bells fashioned from of beer cans to make the tap dancing seem more chthonic and harmonious.

She taught me to be embarrassed for God's sweet sake and possible disapproval. Her husband had already shown his own disapproval by his disappearance act. One night he sneezed and lost his dentures while riding a motorcycle in the street. That was the end of the relationship. My mother edited him right out of her life. Dentures were a sign of God's favor. If you ever lost a set of dentures, even a gold tooth could not save you from the boogie man or bag lady.

What did that matter? Being married to God was a blessing and a curse and at any moment bag ladies and defrocked priests might appear out of the woodwork and demand reticence, and the humility of deaf mutes and a bevy of irritating circus performers. My mother told me, she warned me, she admonished me, she chastised me, never become like what you could become.

Every bone in your body can be broken by a man as well as by god but if you become a bag lady, understand that is even worse and you deserve not a gold sovereign or a copper of god's mercy to be showed upon you in a blessing.

The problem was my mother wanted to become a novelist from the first. If she felt she could write a novel about Mary Magdalene she hid her deepest desires from me. She could have become notoriously famous overnight as if a master riding a rambunctious lion into a Roman Forum or catacomb of voracious delight. Instead, everything was veiled, secret, and hidden and since every story had a shocking ending, the stories' impact began to wane as I grew older. That's when my panic attacks began.

I am not sure whether most people know the secret regarding the elixir of life: the ingredients and recipe for deer musk. Are you aware deer can anticipate gallstone and gallbladder attacks? Unfortunately, many humans have lost this inborn capacity for sensing misfortune is around the corner. It is this loss of powers that have caused civilizations to flounder and squander gold, oil, and end up in squalor and the ashes of the slumbering homeless under the filthy bridges frequented by the disenfranchised.

Have you understood there may be no longer any need for morning and evening? Most people agree to worship the sun but when it comes to the moon, the many unsuspecting mundane people of the world understand or grasp the meaning of blood red moons shining on all of pristine nature during an eclipse. They do not appreciate the multiple reflections of the moon. The illumination of the god-forsaken and the damned and the tormented living under the opprobrium of the shadow-filled devil's scythe. What about them? How would they be saved from my mother's wrath?

My mother used to tell me she was very concerned that I might become blind. She believed that blindness was catching like the ebola virus or tuberculosis. My mother told me that if I played the violin too quickly or too well and if I did not dance well enough, I could never become an opera star and she used as an example not of a Cardozo family member this time but she alluded rather slyly to the scum of the earth, the besotted and unlucky members of the Furioso family whose bloodlines were frayed and rotted at the core due to the dubious roots chewed away by disingenuous dragon ornaments who were allowed to grace and adorn the edges of the childhood cradleboard that kept one's spine straight and one's arms swaddled and out of harm's pernicious way.

Sometimes my mother would tell me every night the story of Ruby, the blind girl, from that unmentionable member of that unremarkable and blemished and tarnished family left with only a small dollop of molasses spread between two of her fingers on either hand to play with. Now this story alluded to the fact here was an exemplary curse embodied in a poor sighted and ugly child, poor girl who had been singled out and condemned to play with a feather or play cat's cradle during the entire length of her and during crooked lengths of star-filled nights to atone for the sins of her grandfather who had refused to play the hammered dulcimer when she was most needed. That's why the wedding of my mother to my father was a disaster. Because of that one incident.

Of course, had the family known her husband would bring such dishonor to the various and sundry members, that the old man would suffer impecunious fates of blackouts reflecting the cards drawn down the night could never turn out right when drawn on her behalf, perhaps they would figure it was fate and the angels that insisted his hammered dulcimer string break at the wedding.

My mother used to warn me in this way: mark my words, daughter, if Harry had opted to have played for my husband's funeral, things might not have been any different. Never mind about Ruby refusing to play at my wedding. Of course, because Harry did not fulfill his contract with God and the angels, it would be no surprise that God and the angels might opt to take him for a photo shoot early and take away his soul from his weakened frame. The only reason Harry might be graced with a long life that kept him more than a few steps away from the grave was due to the little silver vile of whiskey he kept in his back pocket. In addition, cherry cordials and famous liqueurs from the old country were the one reason the angels might deem he was worthy of having the sins washed away from the confines of his body and would let him stay despite the fact he was wearing out his welcome on earth.

I asked for a stone but received neither bread nor meat. I asked for bone but received neither light nor dark. In harvest of first breath, last breath, who follows eternity's dance of death? Among birds releasing candelabra of branches, do you expect the wind to do the rest? These were the words engraved upon my mother's gravestone upon her death in 1942. I was born in 1943. I had to relive her life all over again. I had now to relive my life as her life all over again but now claim the body of Elizabeth Martina Bishop just to do the job. Ah such is life!

Dancing at seven years old and full of purpose

BOOK 3

GRANDMOTHER BIRD

Part I

Old Grandmother Bird,
Does she have anything to tell me?
Is she not the first one who taught me to fly?
Scissor-clipped, her spirit voice undefeated and courageous
A voice drawn down and fed by keening grace notes
Snipped by a kind and undying wind from the north,
Have you ever heard her singing?
I can hear her voice taken up with whispering
Over Canadian territories and the Rockies
Over dark woods of penumbra plumbing the depths
Of Compassion's Holy Spirit?
When I first met her, what if I told her:
I know you? I know you know what happened. Chief Joseph
One among several who agreed to split the face of God and sigh
What of his last breath? Tell me he did not drown.
Tell me he did not die.
What if she told me all in one sitting
The ancestral light of every spirit
Eclipsed by the dark grey wings
Of a single photograph. A photograph
She had been saving all these years,
A photograph encompassing every parabola of love.
That being said, what if she strung through eye-holes of time
A hundred tethered threads, half-sewn,
Embroidered in overlapping leaf-tapestries
Disowned yet owned by a single tribe
Fed by silk yet no more meaning silk
Than the watery tread of invisible ocean
Whose waves never unpin the hair

Of a goddess steering the delight of waves.
Why soften the broken edges of the dark
When finite leaves uncurl fists of tiny tendrils
Unfurling the soft-petunia petals of curlicues of blossom
At evensong and at matins plaintive plainsong chanted

Before I even looked upon the photo your Aunt Wanda
Had so lovingly cured in her hands.
What of her wedding picture suddenly
Fell into ash and left your hands slightly heart-scalded?
What of she told me of a winged consort, a winged lion
Who once guarded a tomb in Gujarat gave up the ghost.
That small chinks of light had gone op against the dark
Moaning mouth of the moon. Did anyone notice
The eye of the moon grew red as a cloak grew along
The hedgerows in the monsoon season.
Grandmother Bird, did you tell no one what you saw?
Who was it, was it you, unpinned the truth
From the core of maple and oak?

Were I to have dreamt the dream in which Pyramis
Herself was slain, would you deny the truth?
Would you and she have been the only ones
Left standing weeping in a sacred grotto openly?

Part II

Whose are these infinite blossoms that blush with the bluish tint
Of breath? O infinite calligraphy of breath that vanishes.
Upon hearing the wind beneath her feet, would she be slain
In spirit? In this point of the story, why does everything
Become unclear and shaped by a sudden longing for tobacco ties?
Was Grandmother Bird laughing or weeping profusely
Unloosing her gospel in pious bouts of blasphemous joy?
What was her reaction to the fevered flesh
Half- whispered asides before the fixings of an altar
Before the makings of an unseen spirit form?
Anasazi, do you hear anyone crying out?
Unheard by any her footfalls echoing on the coast
If these are not yours walking beside me
From one generation to another, please let me know.
Grandfather might have been the one to tell me:
How it must have been, how it might have been for him.

Part III

Grandmother Bird,
Is this the way it has always been for you and for me?
For all the relatives? No one is ever short-changed?
Is this your first time
Hearing this story? Is this all you can say? Yes, this is my first time
Ever hearing the beginning and ending of this story?
Is there no time
For reflection in this life?
Yes, my daughter, the wise ones knew of floods
That were coming. Whose words were these that were spoken?
Whose gourd outpoured with love?
I assure you her voice was love.
In that half dreaming way of hers I heard her tell me:
As the guest of the innkeeper, I have always been blessed.
Blameless in my ignorance, I do not really know his proper name.
Blameless I am as smoke weaving
Among the fitful leaves in autumn.
Grandmother Bird, is this how you express your love in the story?
But when I asked her, she could not tell me. She did not answer.
In the split star seed of the almond tree,
What is the sense you have of yourself?
I have no sense of my own existence.
That much she said, that much of the story recounted.
Then she told me. I cannot look into the eyes of sound.
I cannot taste nor savor my own essence. I cannot only sleep
Until my bones forgot they ever had a body or flew like the rain
On the mountain, I did not know the cause of my coming
To this part of the world.

Part IV

In the farthest realms of the upper worlds, it is said by the elders:
Water will never cease its journey nor drought sully the thoughts
Of those who believe in the quixotic dance of solitary bees.
Instead, the people will be shown the truth: the fact water will run
Past grape vineyards, past the hidden churchyards, wine-cellars,
Cairns and caves until it reaches the possible kingdom
Of Father Sky.

At a certain time, the proper time,
When a young girl is to be placed
In a hollow canoe, no one would ever think
To court her with questions:
Where does she come from? Please do not ask me:
Why has she come?
On no account,
Can she delay or answer questions about the nature
Of the ritual event. On no account, should she leave. The body
Of the birch bark canoe is part of her snowshoe destiny.

The sacrament of the new moon allows
For her birthing to take place.
When the prow of the canoe touches land, she cries out
Before she swims into being enough
To allow for another being to land.
She knows enough not to speak but to remain mute as a stone.
Since earth does not touch the body but her body touches earth
When the boat arrives
Further than the eye can see on a distant shore
She then opens her eyes. How will she know rest?

Part V

If palaces unlocked their leaf-ridden doors, would they measure
Thirty cubits? Possessed by the divine intoxication of a beating
Heart, what do you remember? What garment have you cast off?
What other garment have you assumed as the flesh of your body?
The soul-helmet has so little room. She tells me she has so little
Notion of what actually happened; a
At the time when Joseph cast off his body
He simply vanished. She still asks: what happened to him?
My beloved
Is he not in the next room waiting for me? She tells me she recalls
How in the middle of everything, when he was going, he suddenly
Grew aware of where he was going and commented on the details
Of the rooms of heaven that he would inhabit
After he had left her.
She kept asking him: what do you want? Isn't there something?
But there was nothing. All day she told herself he was not going.
That he could not vanish into thin air.
That they would not take him.
That his body would stay with her as a kind of prayer.
As he was leaving, she told me:
I know he was reaching for something. I wish I knew.
I wish I knew is all she said. Over and over. Wasn't he reaching
For a rafter of smoke? A reed? A jade water jar?
A cave nectar-filled.
His lost uncle. The island where she spent the summers.

As he was passing by, I looked out the window.
I thought I saw a mud turtle

Scribbling a message with his gigantic claws.
I thawed out the meat
I used to use for his favorite Italian wedding soup.
But he would have none of it.
His body was beyond recipes for living and nourishment.
He was almost given over. I was too was given over.
But I didn't know
Whose turn it was to swim into the night sky
To make amends for life's unerring sense of unwritten karma.
As it was, she was always the one who wanted to shy away
From death or anyone who thought to make any mention of it,
Whether in the waning or waxing of moon-driven tides.
Whether the flood waters had driven everyone from their houses,
The thought of death was all the same to me.
Even if Mother Earth
Flattened beyond recognition,
The unnamed memory of mountains
Bore the same name: Mauna Kea.
As soon as the flood waters had receded,
It became clear the features of the town
Now flattened beyond recognition.
Mothers could no longer recognize their children
Nor dogs their owners or the places where they slept.

How was Mother Earth's body created?
How much can I tell you of the story?
From the little I was told, I know her body
Was Called a Canoe like a Chief's House.
How it grew into incarnation
Was only through nourishment by coconut milk,
And offerings of pig entrails.
Grandmother, when will the half story be completed in the quilt
Pattern you are sewing with your own hands? What parts
Of your mother tongue so heart-scalded,
They have cut out your speech?
Do you miss him more than the memory of your grandchildren?

You record how quilt unties its tilted thimbles from the drumbeats
Of your heartfelt testimony.

Who is listening?
Your whole being cries out
For the changes that will come and
None of us will speak of that time.
Is it you who will detail for each of us, bold, death-defying moves
And extraordinary leaps through time.
Who can escape the mark of time?
Regarding the fearless wizardry of stitchery.
In a dream of lightning,
A dream is never done until your words
Make clear the story of your return,
In a dream of her natal return,
How many lives has she lived as her own?
Why did she never tell us
The stories of the Children of Lir
Or the Bald-Faced Liar from Dehra Dun
Or the In the Wake of the Tsunami
Penned by a friend of Maud Gonne's?
Yet, how well she knows swans she knows still linger in a green,
Willow-filled sanctuary
Of narrow fern-lined rivers.

How well she recalls love lies sleeping
Like a newborn faun in such sanctified places.
Like Joseph, she wishes
To drown in god.
If a cup of sorrow were to overturn on the kitchen table,
In a dream of remorse, would she mourn, would she moan?
To what star would she offer her final condolences?
Remember love's eternal dance
At a distance from your soul until you penned these words.

She gets up,
She yawns, she yeans for him and cannot get up for breakfast
In the morning.
She notes the progression of days; in the same way
One day follows upon another.
The sky is a home for a hunchbacked dream.
She can't recall the name of the gate-keeper in her dream.
The red-haired hag keeps quiet about what she has seen.
A humming bird makes an appearance briefly and then is gone.
She still longs to be buried beneath the rooted mysteries of death.

Part VI

If a surgeon's heartbeat beats wildly,
In the way of a hammered dulcimer,
Why stammer or give out a reproof?
Why raise the roof? According to
The druid's music of the muses
Who can prove what is to happen happens next?
Why remain vexed when the words won't come?
Two kinds of forests remain overgrown
One a wooded park another a forest of retorts.
Sunken back into the cauldron of the world.
Is there anywhere in the circus tent
Where it is safe to practice the art of divination?
What of the veils within the veils?
Among the nameless and named forces
Of creation, is there anything left to manifest
That will not derail the art of the imagination?
Has every medicine bundle containing plant medicine
Been left forgotten in the kinship of relatives
What of the elemental forces convening sparrows?
Where dwells the Mother of All Sorrows?
Who was the one who greeted Deganwida and his brothers?
The one who greeted Joseph and the others?
When they passed over each of his warriors relented
And spoke the truth about their lives.
Why bother to repeat what they did so many times?
Is it true they remained unheard until the time they passed?
These are the ones that said: We will fight no more forever.

Part VII

Dressed in the raiments of disconsolate birds
I have seen the kerchiefed elders take off
Before a shining esplanade. Unless honored,
They will refuse to come back up north to check
On their erstwhile relatives left abandoned in the cold.
If man if woman were meant to plight their troth
Beneath the dream-ridden shade of pine trees,
What of Lilith entranced then whose snake-like arms and hands,
Expanded and idled into Shiva-like dalliance of branch and limb?

Why are you then so discomfited when you come to find out
She descended earthbound then when much older,
Hair now silvered with metaphor of snow falling down metaphor?
What shape-shifting guileful and ungrateful woman could imagine
Agape wreathed in flowers sprouting arbutus in every season?

Does life admonish and burn a humbled spirit
For absolutely no reason? Is this her pilgrimage?
Whose are these footsteps peopled with those of grim frowns?
Why spend an entire life paddling up stream,
In the way of a green turtle before he's gentled into sand?
What a fine canoe! Blue Jay says. I've never seen one
Ornamented with white shell, obsidian, and turquoise.

Part VIII

Upon hearing the wind blow, would I be slain in spirit?
Who hears the voices of little leaves burning? What does slain
In spirit mean to the blue canopies of horses who know
What they mean before the wilderness of fallow fields, untilled?

Anasazi, who was the one walking beside you gifting you canoes
Laden with blue corn, white corn,
Red corn and everywhere green leaves
Overflowing when the wind congealing fire in four directions?
Whose visionary spirit out leaps the scroll
Where chickens are dutifully
Sacrificed in Senegal? Circling,
Will the eyes of an ox wind around?
What force will bring you to your senses?
A soundless labyrinth of bells?
Or is the bestial eye of every horse blinkered and turned inward?

I imagine every human tear would turn a mill.
If every woman's eyes
Heavy-lidded, unguessed by a myriad of stars falling into tethered
Unfailing and unfaltering dignity of feathered darkness,
Where will you go to trace supernatural light
Moored in a single storm?

Or have you lost the pathway of the night sky,
The same night sky that steadies the fiery rounds
Of meteors and comets in the precincts of their surround?
Who will straighten the spine of the hunchback?

Hasn't spirit divined within us that mysterious force
We have come to know we cannot understand?
When the rose whispered to the cypress and the juniper,
What news was recited exactly?
Before whose altar does hawk refuse
To bequeath the symmetry of his wings?

Why do you refuse
To open up before a bevy of birds whose swarming oceans
Move into nothingness and, word for word,
Call out for prophets to overturn the salted cup of sky-ocean?

Why heap praises before venomous demons? Why divine words
Before the atonement of silence? What if a tongueless hermit
Spent his life as an idolatrous seer?
Grandmother, what would you do then?

Part IX

These words I remembered as I swam into the ethers of the world.
And yet I remembered little,
Almost nothing of the places I had been
Or the hidden places of the cosmos I claimed I had been.
That's what she said. She asked me: How can I avoid drowning?
How can I meet the one who left so many deeds undone
During seven generations. How can you avoid being old?
Nobody agrees to pull along anyone else alone.
How do you move alone?
How do you sleep
Through the subtle movements of your soul body?
Without telling anyone, your eyelids flutter and close
And still you call yourself part of holy spirit
And all the people you have met.
Are they not lonely for praise songs to be uttered over water?
The water rises upon the landscape. The bowsprit splits apart
The wide open sky. Does your spirit swim through walls of water?
Say I am not I nor you. Say you've never lied
About the meaningful acts of your existence.
Do you persist in running away from the discomfiture
Of your body's body and remarkable good fortune?
Count yourself lucky in still being alive. Why were you so thirsty?
What rendered your ordinary life so meaningful
Or as commonplace as breath? Everyone walks alone.
Mother Earth follows the sun. You are no different
Than anyone else. How come? I am not sure of anything.
That I would not fall under the sway of someone other.
Why make yourself a drunkard
Out of the desire for karma's balance?

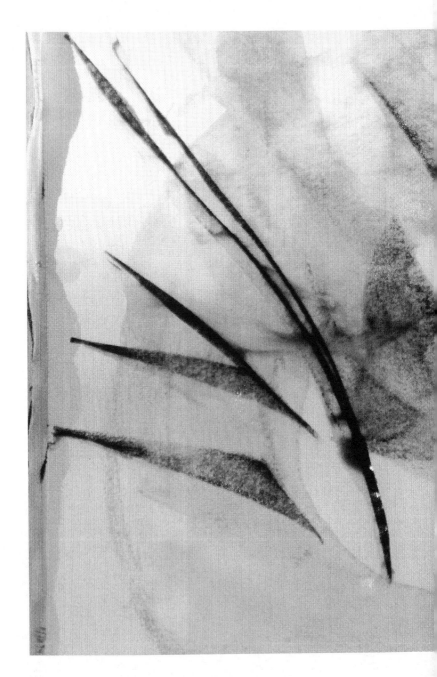

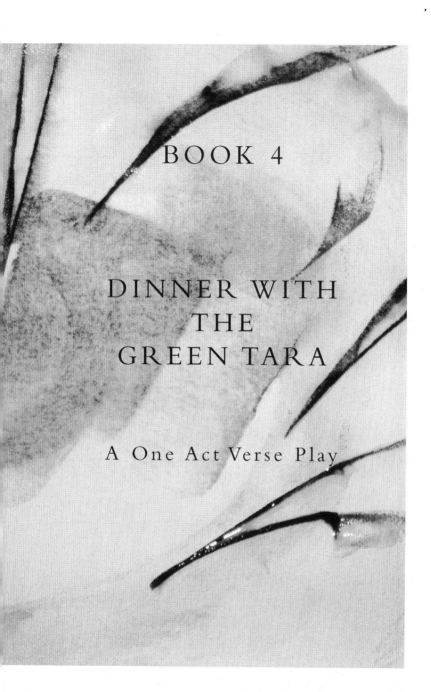

BOOK 4

DINNER WITH THE GREEN TARA

A One Act Verse Play

Dinner With the Green Tara

HE

I cannot bear to look upon your face. I cannot bear to read these new lines etched so deeply across your brow. So different than last year when playing tennis was effortless and you thought you were Martina not Elizabeth.

SHE

How do I know who I am. I have I don't know what kind of identity I have. I am not sure if I ever felt anything about who I am. I mean the body is kind of raw when you grow up asthmatic and your parents grieve your death as if you'd never been born. But when I fell, I hurt my breast. Suddenly, I felt what it was like to have a breast. My breast, my left breast hurt so badly that I knew I had one. All of once, I began to have the sense of who I was, who I am.

HE

You have to see the comedy in all this. Going the wrong way on a gravel path of the night you turn the wrong way and know you're headed in the wrong direction. So then, blind as a bat, you go and fall and you are still laughing and hanging out in the darkened cave of your very existence here on earth. And you die a thousand times even though you have gathered it is not your time. And another guy coming up on his motorcycle just drops the body and that's the end of that and as we near our own extinction, we praise god with a flourish and keep on going. Am I strong enough for the task? The flesh hangs on our skin as if we are to stimy scarecrows.

SHE

I can always make people laugh. And bats too, they are in their cave.

HE

You lied to me. The crucifixion of the moment is the love that you gave.

SHE

But I see it in me. The lies, I mean. I mean I don't want to be martyred. I don't want to be still martyred when I wakeup on the other side and realize I was a suicide.

HE

The book of common prayer. As old as Hester Prynne. That's why you have no teeth. All your life you have lied to too many people until your teeth fell out. Your hair is silvered as in a winter sleet or hail.

SHE

I can count the numbered hairs on my chin but not on my head. But I see it in you. You, as old as Quan Yin. Ave Caesar.

HE

But I don't see it in me. Who I am to topple kingdoms in the sand?

SHE

Do you know how these books are written? I never had any kingdoms in the sand. You look older than I remember. As a pastor, you were younger but you gave me the nod.

HE

I have kingdoms. I live in the void.

SHE

All I do is sit and tell her to sit quiet as the sky before rain has fallen. Like a cigar box Indian she sits without speaking.

HE

Without saying a word? It is hallucination. It is botox with a touch of high cheekbones from the countesses of egypt Bombay or is it Bonn. Is it not verboten to speak of metaphors that are ethnic slams.

SHE

Or of high royalty from which she came. My friend, just look at her. She is in her element now. She has always sat in the void. She hastens to chastise all those who see the dynamic energy streaming from a person's aura. She thinks it is all illusion. She is mightier than a sow and holier than thou. And when she saw people worshipped cows, she withdrew herself from India and though she swore she would never eat meat again, she herself was moritified at her dishonesty.

HE

But the world is all the same. Just because a person wears a turban, he can still tears your lips with his teeth and cause your gums to bleed saying all the while: I know what you need. And I do, you know.

SHE

Know what?

H E

There are all kinds of unambiguous signs you know. Signs of the times, don't you know. The signs of.....What was I thinking of....it is your eyes..you do have lovely eyes. What about her?

S H E

And here you begin to digress and the waiter has given up on us. We shall not consume tea or remain civil or anything that would work. What about her? What do you mean?

H E

Waitress, hold your tongue. Eat water cress and parsley and grow young.

S H E

Well I did drive across America once. Well, of course that was when I was quartered and fed. Most of all I was young. I could imagine things to do with my body like hiking across the Alps. Of course, today people pay other people to use their bodies and walk across a shopping mall with a mindful gait.

H E

Of course that was when you were young. And younger than that and I could walk on all fours. After all, I know you little or no idea I was an Olympic swimmer.

S H E

You wore an Olympic medal or two. Nothing would surprise me. You had it hung about your neck. There were tears in your eyes when you sang god bless America and you were totally undone. You knew once you had the medal, you didn't have to accomplish anything else in your life.

HE

My friends, when I had some decent ones that knew how to share, they made me take the morning shift and I saw god and I knew the symphony I saw was some kind of nod from him.

SHE

I cannot let you know what I am thinking. I cannot even see. I am half blind.

HE

Perhaps legally blind and no doubt without a dog.

SHE

I need a guide that is not a dog. A master perhaps.

HE

Of tax evasion.

SHE

This is all too surreal.

HE

Don't you see I am blushing.

SHE

Like a schoolboy. Yes, you are blushing, rather....The sun is shining.

HE

Well that is a tea party in itself my dear. I have to go home and feed the dogs.

SHE

Is not claustrophobia over the white tea napkins? The dogs must be hyperbolic by now.

HE

No. It is the white gloves the waiters share. Their knowing smiles. Something more like that.

SHE

Be discreet. I see dinner napkins put up across their beard and I know they are spraying.

HE

Spraying, spraying what?

SHE

They are spraying pesticide on my luggage.

HE

To get rid of you and your daughter?

SHE

Because she is black and I am white. And after a while, people don't like to see things like that. Things like parquet floors.

HE

Or is it all because your sister is Indian and you are white?

SHE

But we are both Indians, I think. Except my grandfather washed his clothes one night and it all washed out.

HE

You are both Indian? What are you trying to tell me? A thing like that, you would take care to know. Probably from the beginning of time. There are lots of kudos involved in being like unto the Indians, an Indian. You can get free acreage and things. Identity theft would be harder to come across. You can make box top offers to the blind. You can get free trips to Nassau or Bimini in the Bahamas, go anywhere in the world for the price of half a song. Once your passport is stamped a certain way, you can go anywhere for half fare. Perhaps because you were there first and had a logo printed on your boxer shorts when you ran a marathon. You were there or here first. As the crow flies, is there no singular kind of retort?

SHE

Or, depending on what age you lived in—you would take care not to know. I never asked my mother why all my aunts were black. My uncles bit their knuckles and their never sported beards. They pointed with their chins to indicate the direction of where they were going.

HE

They probably grew crops as a reflection of the position of the sun. And they kneel like Egyptians in the desert when the blue corn rises with the sun.

SHE

The sun rises and the sun sets but we die alone.

HE

Turtle demon. You roll your eyes and what do you see. We die alone and of the cold winters we do not see or the heat. Trust me on this, Trust me.

SHE

I trust no one. I know no days and no nights. I swim in the ethers alone.

Books by Elizabeth Martina Bishop

Elizabeth has published more than 30 poetry collections.
All books available through Amazon.com.
Here is a small selection of her work.

Praise Song for a Dab Chick

When dab chicks are first set out to pasture they may be resistant to various archetypal states of individuation, and integration.
While surrendering to a gradual blending into nature, including the terraced garden plot, the orchard, the tree as well as underbrush, dab chicks eventually gain strength and learn to lean into the angled brightness of flying.
Author Elizabeth Bishop tells us specifically the dab chicks are just excuses for the imagination to enjoy earth's biosphere as well as the transformative voice of nature poetry.

ISBN-13: 978-1492893837 • ISBN-10: 1492893838 • $11.95

As Long As We Both Shall Dance

Not sure what to do today? Meditate on a Tarot card and find a new sense of direction.
The studies on the Tarot cards offered in the pages of this book may inspire you to make a shamanic excursion into the vast, unknown worlds of poetic endeavor and fantasy.
When using your imagination, the choices you make on the path to self-realization offer new lessons that may later lead you towards a more formal study of the Tarot.

ISBN-13: 978-1493592722 • ISBN-10: 1493592726 • $14.95

Honoring the Elders

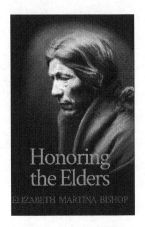

Many of the poems in this collection honor the elders and anticipate the enjoyment of the natural world.

Restoring the importance of Mother Earth and reclaiming her power is central to the premise of this collection of talk stories and poems.

First Peoples were never to be separated from Mother Earth. At the point of colonial contact, the rights of the people were violated.

We are to remember we are all interconnected, no matter what. Much healing and honoring needs be accorded ancestral ways, now and forever.

ISBN-13: 978-14993699261 • ISBN-10: 1493699261 • $11.95

Second Sight

These poems reflect the author's continued engagement with her contemplation of nature and its blessed surround.

Communing with nature is what calls forth a healing poetic response.

The inner paradise of contemplative thought may be the only paradise on earth. Please read these poems aloud and enjoy the metaphorical palette..

ISBN-13: 9781494402129 • ISBN-10: 1494402122 • $9.95

Upon Reaching
A Foreign Shore

A sudden leap of consciousness.
A leap of faith.
Karma is an open door.

A way of attending to the spiritual nature of the writing discipline. This is what poet Elizabeth Martina Bishop is all about.

She leaves the door open for readers to enter into new ways of thinking about the natural world. Even within the postmodern urban context, the inner dance remains the same.

ISBN-13: 978-1494739805 • ISBN-10: 1494739801 • $9.95

Cosmic Excuse

Poetry contains a recipe within it.
A dash of salt, a dash of wisdom's soul.

These poems reflect the poets' continued interest in nature blended with spiritual insight that makes the listeners' spirit want to dance and celebrate life.

ISBN-13: 978-1495247651 • ISBN-10: 1495247651 • $9.95

Camille's Return

Camille's Return consists of a series of short laconic poems about inner and outer transformational states. To remain conscious and acutely aware of the cosmos and all the transcendent changes taking place, poetry can serve as a mediating borderland of consciousness. Poetry mediates inner realms implicating the shameless mysterious interplay between light and dark. Each poem may be considered a talk story that mesmerizes and leads readers towards the pathway of holistically inspired memoir. Memories of past, present, and future lives are not left out in the cold. Poetry charts the heart's return to grace.

ISBN-13: 978-1496123718 • ISBN-10: 1496123719 • $9.95

Dreaming of Karmic Birds

The golden birds of karma let us fly free from old constraints and emerge into shimmering sunlight.

Life reviews invoked by the discipline of meditation can lead to new vistas of expanded consciousness and enjoyment of the path of metaphor and poetry.

ISBN-13: 978-1497416093 • ISBN-10: 1497416094 • $13.95

Goats Descending a Mountain

These poems are experimental in form. Goats Descending a Mountain shows the way in which improvisational forms can ignite mindful steps enabling pathways towards awakening of the imagination, inspiration, and courage.

ISBN-13: 978-1497586512
ISBN-10: 1497586518 • $9.95

Maiden from Mullingar

The Stories:
Irish traveller tales are some of the oldest remnants of traditional oral culture. These stories have been recorded and adapted from original travelers the author met on the roads of rural Ireland. In addition to these tales, this book offers a poetic smorgasbord of Irish culture.

The Background:
With the disappearance of many itinerant crafts today is born a new integration honoring the old craft of story telling. These days, we can appreciate time-honored traditions that invite readers to enter a transcendent dreamtime. Such an invitation is always present for those who risk a continuous pilgrimage.

That is the fearless way of the traveling people who constantly evoke an old way of life that has been displaced by emigration and industrial development. These fictional stories and poems mirror archetypal realities as well as anthropological portraits.

ISBN-13: 978-1499321968 • ISBN-10: 1499321961 • $ 11.95